CHRISTOPHER PALLES

CHRISTOPHER PALLES

LORD CHIEF BARON
OF
HER MAJESTY'S COURT OF EXCHEQUER
IN IRELAND
1874—1916

His Life and Times

By
V. T. H. DELANY

1960
ALLEN FIGGIS & CO., LTD.
DUBLIN

MADE AND PRINTED IN THE
REPUBLIC OF IRELAND BY
CAHILL AND CO., LTD., DUBLIN

CONTENTS

CONTENTS

PREFACE

FORTY years have now elapsed since Christopher Palles died. He was the last of the Barons of the Exchequer and the greatest of the Irish judges. During that time much has happened in Ireland and there have been manifold changes in the country's social and political structure. Continuity has been maintained at but few points, one of them being the legal system operating there. Political changes have, it is true, raised legal problems; but the basis of the system remains unchanged.

It is a real tragedy that some contemporary did not write of the Chief Baron, for the passage of nearly half a century has dimmed the recollections of some, while others who could have thrown light on his life and character are no longer with us. Accordingly, it is with considerable diffidence that I attempt to give some account of his career and his work in the law. Most lawyers are familiar with Palles the judge; few know anything of Palles the man, and it is this lacuna that I have attempted to fill. There is included a chapter on his legal work, but it may safely be ignored by those who are not concerned with such things.

My task was greatly lightened by the inspiration of my friend, Dr. A. G. Donaldson, whose idea it was that a Palles biography should be written, who had done much to clear the ground, and who stimulated me to undertake the work. Without his encouragement and erudition this book would never have been written. To him I am most deeply grateful.

In my quest for information I have received help from many people. If I do not mention them all by name it is only because I fear that an exhaustive list might inadvertently omit some of my friends. My thanks must go to Mrs. Irma Waddell, the Chief Baron's grand-niece, through whose kindness I was given free access to the Palles family papers, and whose personal recollections of him, enjoyed by me in such hospitable surroundings, shed illumination

on many a dark place. I must also express my gratitude to
Mr. R. A. French, who made certain documents available
to me, and to Mr. Joseph Kennedy, himself a kinsman of
the Chief Baron, who was so patient in answering my
many queries.

My thanks, too, must be extended to the Hon. Mr.
Justice Barry; the Hon. W. E. Wylie, Q.C.; the Hon.
W. B. Black, S.C.; the Hon. Mr. Justice Kingsmill Moore;
Mr. W. H. Carson, Q.C.; Mr. Henry Moloney, S.C.;
Mr. Peter Duggan; Mrs. A. Kavanagh, and Miss
E. F. K. McCormick for personal recollections; to
Revd. Father Bagot, S.J., then Rector of Clongowes
Wood College, for his patient searches in the College
archives; to Dr. Séamus Wilmot, Registrar of the
National University of Ireland, and Miss Ellen Power,
Librarian of University College, Dublin, for help in con-
nection with the Chief Baron's educational work; to the
Benchers of the Honourable Society of King's Inns,
Dublin, for allowing me to search their records; to Mr. W.
Holden, M.B.E., Librarian of Gray's Inn; Mr. K. Howard
Drake and the staff of the Institute of Advanced Legal
Studies; Professor Mark de Wolfe Howe, of the Harvard
Law School; the staff of the Yale Law School Library;
and Mr. T. P. O'Neill, of the National Library of Ireland,
for bibliographical assistance; to Professor R. Dudley
Edwards, Dr. R. B. McDowell, F.T.C.D., and my colleague, Professor J. C. Beckett, for giving me the benefit
of their expert knowledge of the nineteenth century;
to Miss Helen Taylor, for her skilful and painstaking typo-
graphy; and to my wife, for undertaking once more the
task of proof-reading and indexing.

Of those who are no longer with us, I recall with
pleasure my conversations about the Chief Baron with
Serjeant A. M. Sullivan, Q.C., himself the last survivor of
an extinct order, whose wealth of recollection and melli-
fluous diction did much to lighten my work and gladden
my heart.

I am particularly grateful to the Queen's University of
Belfast, not only for permitting me to consult certain

papers, but also whose generosity in a tangible way both eased the burden of an itinerant researcher and made publication of this book possible.

Finally, I owe much to my colleague, Professor F. H. Newark, C.B.E., and to my friend, Mr. Dermot O'Neill, both of whom read the entire book in manuscript, and whose steady counsel and sound learning often enabled me to avoid the pitfalls of the amateur biographer. If there are errors, they are my responsibility, not theirs.

V. T. H. Delany.

Faculty of Law,
The Queen's University of Belfast.

CHRONOLOGY

25th December, 1831:	Christopher Palles born, second son of Andrew Palles and his wife, Eleanor Plunkett.
23rd November, 1847:	Matriculated at Trinity College, Dublin.
Trinity Term, 1849:	Admitted a student of King's Inns, Dublin.
Hilary Term, 1851:	Admitted a student of Gray's Inn.
Michaelmas Term, 1852:	Graduated Bachelor in Arts, with Senior Moderatorship in Mathematics and Physics.
Hilary Term, 1853:	Called to the Bar. Joined the Home Circuit.
5th August, 1862:	Married Ellen Doyle.
27th April, 1863:	Christopher the younger born.
8th February, 1865:	Called to the Inner Bar.
16th February, 1872:	Appointed Solicitor-General.
15th April, 1872:	Elected a Bencher of King's Inns, and declined.
5th November, 1872:	Appointed Attorney-General.
16th February, 1874:	Appointed Lord Chief Baron of the Court of Exchequer.
22nd June, 1885:	Ellen Palles died.
1892:	Sworn of the Privy Council of England.
5th July, 1916:	Resigned from the office of Lord Chief Baron.
14th February, 1920:	Died at Mountanville House, Dundrum, Co. Dublin.
2nd January, 1953:	Christopher the younger died.

xii

I

THE LEGEND OF CHRISTOPHER PALLES

There is a innate pleasure in emphasising the continuity
between what we are doing and what has been done. An
excessive desire to dwell upon things past has been the
besetting vice of the Irish temperament, and although it
can never be said with too much emphasis that the present
has a right to conduct its own affairs so far as it can, it
ought always to be remembered that continuity with the
past is not a duty, but merely a necessity.

In Ireland, the social and political changes of the past
forty years have brought in their train corresponding
changes in the Irish way of life. An independent parliamentary democracy, tempered in the fires of a revolution,
has sought to throw off the past, or, at least, to select
those aspects of the past which accord with its political
philosophy. It has become unfashionable to dwell on the
way of life current before the establishment of the new
State and, indeed, the whole tenor of events has been an
endeavour to obliterate the memory of its very existence.
As the years pass the number of those who remember the
old Ireland rapidly diminishes and soon they will be no
more. In one respect only has real continuity been preserved, in the application of the principles of the common
law.

One of the most remarkable features of the legal system
which operates in both parts of the island of Ireland is its
extreme flexibility. The common law of England, a collection of semi-barbarian customs, worked out for the
governance of a rather primitive agricultural community,
has been carried to the uttermost ends of the earth and
has been adapted to suit the most diverse needs and circumstances. In the urban civilisation of North America, in
the new political entities on the continent of Africa, people

have come to regard themselves as being the inheritors of the common law, which they regard as being eminently suited to their particular manifestation of democracy. The system may have had to be remoulded to suit new conditions, but its broad principles and its essential aspirations endure. In no country is this phenomenon more striking than in Ireland, where nearness to England, and the historical ties binding the islands together, have rendered it almost inevitable.

A visitor to Gandon's noble Four Courts in Dublin, or to the new Royal Courts of Justice in Belfast, will be made aware of this perpetuation of the legal system. The common law of England, introduced into Ireland in the twelfth century and developed through its own peculiar method of judicial precedent, is still applied in Dublin and Belfast as it was two centuries ago. Even the external form of the courts remains unchanged; the judges in their robes, the barristers in their wigs, and the dignified ceremonial accompanying the public administration of justice, all testify to the fact that here is no new departure, but the repetition of a solemn act having its roots in the remotest past. It is significant, indeed, that soon after the establishment of the Irish Free State, a Government Commission charged with the task of recommending changes in the existing judicial system, while reminded in their terms of reference that that system was " a standing monument of alien government," and that they should approach their task " untrammelled by any regard to any of the existing systems of judicature," were content to advocate reforms which, while they altered the purely formal structure of the courts, left the essential foundations intact. A body of laws with such a history was not easily supplanted and it is to the credit of that Commission that the great corpus of the common law survived. Attacks upon the courts and upon systems of law are nothing more than an expression of unrest, seeking to deny the necessity for law and order. When the ignorant are taught to doubt they do not know what they safely may believe. What is most important in the new Ireland is education in the significance of existing institutions, not investigation of obscure ideas.

It is only natural that the common law, operating as it does through an inductive system of prior decision, should place a weighty emphasis upon history and tradition. The fact that a matter has been decided in a particular way in the past is an argument against changing it in the present instance. The law has its history and its heroes, its written records and its unwritten traditions. In every part of the globe to which the common law has been brought, great lawyers have arisen, lawyers who are said to epitomise the excellence and rationality of the system. The parent country has Bracton, Coke, Nottingham, Blackstone, Mansfield and Eldon. The United States of America numbers amongst its legal heroes Marshall, Story, Holmes and Brandeis. In Ireland, the issue is never really in doubt. There, the common law has had its distinguished luminaries, but from the time when in the apocryphal words of Matthew Paris, Henry II held council at Lismore " where the laws of England were by all freely received and confirmed with due solemnity," there has been but one master. That master was Christopher Palles, the last Lord Chief Baron of the Court of Exchequer.

To have outstripped the allotted span of life by some eighteen years, to have occupied the judicial Bench for nearly half a century, these are things which, in themselves, call for comment in an age which mistakenly prides itself in the illusion that change is the hallmark of progress. A long life and an extended tenure of judicial office, however, are insufficient, without more, to confer upon their possessor the title of master of the common law. What is so remarkable about Christopher Palles is that his memory has all but achieved immortality. Wherever the principles of that law are expounded, his name is mentioned as the one who, above all others, represented its very embodiment.

Inevitably, such adulation has its reaction, and the reputation of Palles has undergone frequent changes of fortune. At present, indeed, it may be said that, in Ireland, it is fashionable in some quarters to disparage his legal learning. This is as it should be. There can be no greater tribute paid to his memory than to say that, more than forty years after his departure from the Bench, the soundness of his legal views should still be the subject-matter of active discussion amongst lawyers. In reality, this is akin to true immortality. Palles has not died. His pronouncements of the principles of the common law are still living issues, not dead words to be spelled out from the faded pages of the law reports. In 1939, the English Court of Appeal could still speak of " his great authority," while in 1955 the Lord Chief Justice of England, Lord Goddard, was able to reaffirm the position of Palles in the hierarchy, and to state that his judgments " are still received in that country with the highest respect." In Ireland, there is no ambiguity in the question: " What does the Chief Baron say on the point?" There was only one Chief Baron, for he was the last and the greatest of all the barons.

This book is a belated attempt to give an account of the public career and private life of Christopher Palles. In embarking on his task, the writer is conscious of the fact that it was not as a lawyer alone that Palles achieved eminence. As an exponent of higher education for his fellow-countrymen, as a stabilising influence in the community and, above all, as a Christian gentleman, he is worthy of the attention of posterity. He was born when Catholic Emancipation was but two years old, and he died when the crossing of the Atlantic Ocean by air was an accomplished fact. At the time of his birth the great mass of the Irish people were stricken with poverty and ignorance, and as yet unversed in the exercise of their new-found political rights. When he died the greater part of the island stood on the threshold of complete political autonomy, and within a few months of his passing, most of the institutions to which he had owed his lifelong loyalty were swept away.

A life which spanned such a vital period in Ireland's story stood witness to many changes, and it cannot be pretended that Palles would have approved of those which followed immediately upon his death. One ventures to think, however, that he would have taken comfort in the survival of his first and only love, the common law, and that if he were with us today he would apply its principles in a new Four Courts and under a new dispensation with the same spirit of justice and the same mastery of principle as before.

II

BEGINNINGS

THE change in architectural taste which took place in Dublin during the last thirty years of the eighteenth century, evolving the form which we now term Georgian, reveals few better examples of its later development than that area of the north side of the city which embraced the Gardiner estate. The first Luke Gardiner built Henrietta Street (in which King's Inns now stands), and he was the founder of a family which soon owned a very large part of the city east of Capel Street. The second Luke Gardiner, who became Lord Mountjoy, expanded his estate through Denmark Street and Gardiner's Place to Mountjoy Square and Great Charles Street, while the great avenue joining Mountjoy Square with the Custom House at Beresford Place was partly built by the end of the century. In the square itself most of the houses, except the east side, had been built by the date of the Union, and it was finished a few years later.

Today, sad to relate, many of these magnificent dwellings have decayed into crumbling tenements, though it is to the credit of the authorities that in a number of instances, the fabric has been restored and used to provide modest accommodation for Dublin dwellers. Standing at the corner of Mountjoy Square and looking south, one glimpses a tantalising vista of Gandon's Custom House, from this angle unobscured by the hideous ironwork of the railway bridge. The spacious length of Gardiner Street separates the observer from Custom House and river, the view flanked on either side by the warm red brick—many of them, happily, showing signs of recent restoration. It was at Number 5, Lower Gardiner Street that Christopher Palles was born, on Christmas Day, 1831, the third son of Andrew

Christopher Palles, an attorney and solicitor in the city of Dublin, and of Eleanor Plunkett, his wife.

At the time of Christopher's birth, Andrew Palles was in the course of establishing himself in his profession. He had been admitted to practice in 1824 and he was in his thirtieth year. In addition to the profession of the law, he possessed a considerable landed property in the county Cavan, Mount Palles, near the village of Mountnugent, and it appears that the family spent a part of each year residing there. In 1828 Andrew had married his wife and their eldest child, also named Andrew, was born in 1829. Then followed James, who died in infancy, and the birth of the future Chief Baron was succeeded by that of James Ambrose, who died at the age of twenty-six, Elizabeth, who died un-married in 1872, and Marcella, who married Columbus Drake, of Roriston, county Meath, and who survived until 1913.

Although the Palles family had been seated in the county Cavan since the end of the seventeenth century, their earlier ancestors had their closest associations with Dublin. The name is not an Irish one in origin, and an investigation of the family history reveals the interesting fact that the first of the line to come to Ireland was no less a personage than a Papal legate who afterwards became Archbishop of Armagh. This was Octavian de Palatio, a native of Lombardy, who appears in Ireland before 1477, and who obtained a rescript from Pope Sixtus IV on 19th April of that year, empowering him to assume jurisdiction in the see of Armagh, in opposition to a rival candidate, Edmund Connesburgh, whose claims were being supported by the Crown and the English bishops. The dispute was eventually resolved in 1478, and Octavian was confirmed in his appointment to the see. The name " de Palatio " was apparently derived from the fact that Octavian had been employed in the curial office in the apostolic palace. His surname, de Spinellis, indicates that he was probably the nominee of the merchants of the Florentine banking house of Spinelli.

The family was prominent in the international diplomacy

of the early sixteenth century. Thomas Spinelli was Henry VIII's ambassador in Flanders, and other members of the family are mentioned as bankers in his private letters. No link between this Thomas and Octavian has been found, but it has been suggested that Sixtus IV sent the latter to Ireland in 1477, hoping that his banking connections would make it easier for him to put the finances of the see of Armagh in order.

Octavian de Palatio ruled the archdiocese for over thirty-five years, dying in 1513. He seems to have been a man of considerable wisdom and learning and it has been alleged (possibly without foundation) that it was to him that Fynes Moryson alluded when, treating of the primitive habits of the native Irish, he said:

> "An Italian Friar coming of old into Ireland, and seeing at Armach this their diet and the nakednesse of the women, is said to have cried out:—
>> 'Civitas Armachana, Civitas vana
>> Carnes crudae, mulieres nudae.
>> Vaine Armach city, I did thee pity,
>> Thy meate's rawness, and women's nakednesse.' "

It appears, moreover, from the contemporary evidence of his episcopate that Octavian was not alone in his mission to Ireland, and that he sought to advance members of his family within the Armagh diocese. There is a reference to one of his proctors at the Roman court, Antonius de Palatio, a merchant of Florence, who was with him in the Armagh archdiocese, and in 1499, Octavian relinquished the living of Heynystown to one John de Palatio, subdeacon and canon of Armagh, who is buried in the churchyard of Termonfeckin, where his grave was still visible fourteen years ago. There was also an Alexander de Palatio who was beneficed in the southern part of the archdiocese, and who was rector of Dundalk in 1518, and Andrew, a brother of Octavian, in whom the line was continued. The seal of Archbishop Octavian was formerly preserved in the Public Record Office in Dublin, but was destroyed in 1922. His burial place is at the church of St. Peter, Drogheda. In an interesting document preserved amongst the Palles family papers, and written in the hand of the Chief Baron's father, it is noted that "Octavian displayed a dislike for the Irish of Ulster, and preferred to reside within the Pale."

The family of de Palatio seems to have continued in Ireland and the next member of which there is any record is John, whose will, dated 3rd March, 1562, was formerly preserved in the Court of Probate. He used the anglicised form of the family name, Palles, and his will referred to the fact that he married one Alison Saumarz. He lived in High Street, Dublin, carrying on the business of a banker and goldsmith there. His son, Alexander, appears to have been a man of wealth and position in the city, being a member of the Corporation and Sheriff in 1595.

Successive generations continued to live in Dublin, inter-marrying with the better-known families of the Pale, and names such as Tyrell, Malone, and Read occur in this connection. An earlier Andrew was outlawed with his brother, William, after the rebellion of 1641, being described as "of Cloncavat in the county of Cavan," and his son was the first Palles to bear the name of Christopher. This Christopher died in 1683 and his heir, yet another Andrew, married Mary Plunkett, co-heiress of the Honourable Ignatius Nugent, fifth son of the first Earl of Westmeath. The Plunketts of Dunsaughly were related to the oldest families of the Pale, Mary being descended from Lord Killeen, afterwards Earl of Fingall (of which house the Plunketts of Dunsany and Rathmore were branches). By the middle of the eighteenth century the family was established at Mount Palles, this property having been in-herited through Mary Nugent.

The history of the family, indeed, is quite a normal one, and indicates the various changes in fortune of those who adhered to the ancient faith. During the period of the penal laws, the family papers throw an interesting light on the condition of Roman Catholic landowners under that un-happy system. There are instances of county Cavan neigh-bours entering into collusive "discoveries" in order to enable the Palles family to retain its lands; and there are

also records of some of the members of the family con-
forming to the Established Church with the object of
keeping their property and position. On the whole, the
story is an honourable one, first as property owners and,
later, as the penal laws were relaxed, in the army and in
the professions. The Chief Baron's grandfather served in
the army during the American War of Independence and
also in India. By his wife, Elizabeth, a daughter of Richard
More O Ferrall of Balyna, in county Kildare, was born
Andrew, the Dublin solicitor.

. . . .

The year in which Christopher Palles was born, 1831,
was a singularly unpropitious one in the affairs of the
country. Catholic Emancipation, which had come in 1829,
was obviously an incomplete measure; and it would only
have been a success if it had been administered in a liberal
and humane spirit. This the Government of the day resolutely refused to do. In theory, Protestant ascendancy had
been replaced by equality, and every office, save that of
Lord Lieutenant and Lord Chancellor, had been thrown
open to the Catholics. In practice, the situation remained
unchanged. The Government did little to give effect to the
provisions of the relieving Act. O'Connell was not raised
to the rank of King's Counsel; the Catholics were excluded
from the Bench and the magistracy, and the Chief Secretary,
Stanley, did nothing to remove the twin grievances of the
Irish majority—adequate provision for the Catholic clergy,
and the injustice of the tithe. In 1832, it is true, Grey's
Government introduced a measure of parliamentary reform
in Ireland, but the franchise remained at a high level and
the forty shilling freeholders, who had been deprived of
their position in 1829, were not restored.

Perhaps the most important measure of reform introduced was in the field of education. A Board of Education
had been formed in 1806; and Peel, when Chief Secretary,
had done much to remove some of the anomalies of the
system. At the same time, the evangelical movement had

turned its attention to Ireland, and a number of societies of a proselytising character had been formed with the object of furthering its aims. They were followed by another organisation, the Kildare Place Society, which, it must be said, made a very real effort to bring secular instruction to the young Catholics of Ireland. Its attitude towards biblical study, however, soon brought it under the ban of the Catholic clergy, and when Grey took office the primary education of the country was in a most imperfect state.

The solution was found in the " National " system, introduced by Stanley in 1831. Schools were to be established throughout the country to which children of the poorer classes might resort without fee. Secular instruction was to be given by teachers appointed by the State, while religious instruction was to be left in the hands of the various denominations. The aim was to remove the twin evils of proselytism and sectarian strife and, despite an opposition which continued for almost twenty years and which emanated from the clergy of both the Catholic and Presbyterian churches, the schools provided a sound system of primary education. All these controversies which raged in Ireland between 1831 and 1855 cannot have failed to make a profound impression on the youthful Palles; and there is little doubt that the views on the subject which he held in later life and which he expressed so forcibly, both in public and private, were coloured by these early experiences.

The other grievance of the Catholics, the tithe, was contested with extreme bitterness and during the years preceding 1838 it can be said that Ireland was more disturbed than it had been at any time since the 1798 rebellion. Collisions of a fatal nature between the police and military and the armed peasantry occurred frequently, and the events at Newtownbarry, Carrickshock, and other places, are familiar to every student of affairs in nineteenth century Ireland. The efforts of the law to collect the hated tithe were completely frustrated, and the parallel efforts of those who sought a measure of reform in Parliament had no more success. O'Connell's agitation so alarmed the Government that by a virtual compact with the Melbourne administration, whereby the Liberator agreed to shelve the question of Repeal, the Government in turn agreed to commute the tithe and to reform the municipal corporations. This they did with honour. For the first time, real effect was given to the Emancipation Act. Catholics were admitted to the magistracy and a number became Law Officers of the Crown. In 1836, Michael O'Loghlen, who had been appointed Attorney-General in the previous year, was raised to the Court of Exchequer: in 1837 he became Master of the Rolls, and in 1838 he received a baronetcy. O'Loghlen was the first Catholic to hold judicial office since the reign of Elizabeth I, if one excepts the years of the short reign of James II. By an interesting coincidence, his son, Sir Colman O'Loghlen, was responsible for the legislation in 1867, throwing the office of Lord Chancellor of Ireland open to Catholics.

The effect of this policy of conciliation on the upper and middle classes in the country was considerable, and since O'Connell exerted his influence in restoring law and order, the ultimate result was entirely beneficial. The constabulary force was reorganised on a national basis in 1836, and the influence of the Under-Secretary, Thomas Drummond, was exerted to produce a true level of equality in every department of affairs. He suppressed the Ribbonmen and the Orangemen with ruthless impartiality, and although his reminder to the Tipperary landlords that property had its duties as well as its rights may have made him unpopular with them, this period of nineteenth century Irish history can be regarded as the brightest in a uniformly gloomy scene. Tithe commutation came in 1838 and municipal reform two years later and though the Melbourne government fell after 1841, it left behind it much in the way of solid achievement.

The young Palles grew up in this atmosphere of strife and momentous public events, and it can be imagined that

the happenings of the day were reflected in the views of
the family circle. In maturity he became a staunch Whig
and we may believe that he derived from his father those
principles which were allied with a profound respect for
property, law and order, and which were such a striking
feature of his character.

Of his childhood, no record remains, and it can only be
concluded that he lived in the usual atmosphere of a comfortable middle-class Catholic family. The events already
described, and the rising Repeal agitation of 1842-1844
culminating in the débâcle at Clontarf and the trial of
O'Connell, must have impressed themselves on his youthful
mind. We do not know. We do know, however, that he
was put to school at the age of eleven when, together with
his brother Andrew, he was sent to Clongowes Wood
College, in county Kildare.

At that time, Clongowes had been in existence for almost
thirty years. The members of the Society of Jesus who had
embarked on the formidable task of conducting a comprehensive school for Catholics at a time of extreme political
hostility, could already look back with pride on their
achievements, for the school had in that short period
acquired a most impressive reputation. At the time of the
Emancipation Act, it was feared that efforts would be
made to suppress the religious orders in Ireland, including
the Jesuits, and this is evidenced by the fact that a number
of petitions were presented to the House of Lords that
Clongowes might be spared. It is significant, too, that the
petition emanating from the gentry of the county Kildare
was signed by Richard More O'Ferrall and Ambrose
O'Ferrall, both maternal relatives of Andrew Palles. Their
close interest in the school and their approval of the way
in which it was being conducted may well have influenced
Andrew to send his boys there.

In the first prospectus issued from Clongowes, in 1814,
the Rector, Father Kenney, modestly observed that it did
not " seem necessary " to detail therein the plan of education employed by the Society. This system was, of course,
the *Ratio Studiorum* of the Jesuits, and it may be of

interest to indicate the way of life of the average school-boy at Clongowes in 1843, when the Palles boys became pupils there.

As might be expected, life was hard and rigorous, but it was not entirely without its compensations. The school year extended from 7th September to 31st July. Parents, indeed, were reminded that " the progress and happiness of the young student " required that he should not be removed even at the time of vacation. The school day began at half past five in the morning, with the concession of an extra half hour in bed in winter, and continued until half past eight at night. The general plan of education was that the pupil entered on classical studies at the age period between ten and eleven years, and these studies extended over four years. Mathematical and physical sciences came later and were studied concurrently, extending over one or two years, and bringing the pupil up to the age of eighteen. These were accompanied by a course in logic, psychology and ethics. Chemistry and physics were taught at Clongowes as early as 1821, and just about the time the Palles brothers arrived there the experimental side of the sciences was undergoing a considerable expansion. Christopher's innate aptitude for mathematics was stimulated by his school experiences, and his later brilliance in this department of learning stemmed from that time.

It seems that there were complaints about the spartan regime imposed on Andrew and Christopher, for on 25th September, 1843, Mrs. Palles wrote to the Rector, Father Haly, in these terms:—

"Mr. Palles wished me to write to you to say that he would be glad if you would allow our boys to sleep a little longer in the morning than they do; after this winter they will not find getting up so early so hard; also he would wish they should both learn drawing, Andrew certainly has a taste for it, as to Christopher it remains to be tried, and if after the first quarter he does not seem to succeed in it, he can discontinue; but it is worth a trial."

Life at Clongowes must indeed have been austere after

the comforts of No. 25, Mountjoy Square, where the Palles family was now living; and there may have been justification for this parental appeal. Still, there were lighter moments. At a time when organised school sport was still in a rudimentary state, Clongowes possessed its own football game, played on a gravel pitch, which dated from the early eighteen thirties. Special rules were evolved for this most interesting pastime, which survived until the Rugby code was introduced at the school, around 1888. The important event of the year was the " Grand Matches " played on St. Patrick's Day, and in after life the Chief Baron used to recall that for every goal scored that day there was an extra pancake at dinner for the scorer, with the thoughtful proviso that a boy could transfer his extra pancakes to his friends!

There were other sports, too. Fencing and boxing formed part of the curriculum, while fishing in the Liffey and the coursing of greyhounds by the senior boys were outdoor diversions. On public days and " play days ", the school uniform was worn—a cap made of rabbit skin, a blue cloth coat with brass buttons, yellow cashmere waistcoat and corduroy trousers. Later, this was varied by the substitution of a blue cap and waistcoat, with grey trousers. By 1850 the uniform had become obselete and a picturesque custom was abandoned.

The Palles boys prospered in their studies. A letter dated 5th October, 1844, and written by Andrew to his father deserves to be quoted in full, for it indicates the serious way in which they were approaching the business of learning : —

My dear Papa,
    When I received your first letter I had no idea you were so anxious to hear from us. There is no class of German as yet, but if there are boys to learn it they will get a master. I wish very much you would let me learn it instead of Greek which I *heartily* detest and find very hard, besides that when I am a man I will have very little to do with it; I do not know why such pains is taken to teach it to us when there are several other languages of much greater importance to know that are not taught

at all, while we are spending all our time bothering our heads about Greek. As for Mathematics there are two classes of these, but only for boys that know their Arithmetic perfectly, which I think is great nonsense for Arithmetic is a thing that a person must be constantly attending to remember well and if you leave it off for any length of time you will forget it, and then all your time will be spent in vain. Whereas if one learned both at the same time you would remember them much better.

None of the boys are allowed to learn Chemistry except the three higher schools. I wish you would write an answer to this letter as soon as *possible,* as I am very anxious to know what you intend to have me do. The retreat begins Sunday evening and ends on Wednesday.

I remain, dear Papa,

Your most affectionate son,

A. Palles.

Such views on education from a fifteen year old schoolboy were surprisingly mature, and it seems that both Andrew and his brother were applying themselves to their studies with assiduity. From the school records, it appears that Christopher was a careful if not a brilliant scholar. In the " Order of Composition " for 1846, which ruled the precedence of the pupils in their classes, he was placed fourth, as " second praetor " in the Class of Poetry. In 1845-1846 he was an active member of the " Historical Debating Society," being *proxime accessit* to the medallist in the debates of the year. As the debate silver medal was always regarded as the chief college prize, this was a notable achievement by a boy of his age.

.   .   .   .   .   .

In the ordinary course of events, the brothers would have remained at Clongowes until their eighteenth year but, as we shall see, Andrew left school in 1845, while Christopher did so in 1847, when he was not yet sixteen. This premature termination of his school career is probably to be explained by the happening of a serious family crisis, to which it now becomes necessary to advert.

In the library at Clongowes there is preserved a printed

document, in the form of a petition, dated 3rd June, 1847, in which Andrew Palles prayed that the Lord Chancellor might be pleased to restore his name to the rolls as a solicitor of the Court of Chancery. A perusal of this faded paper reveals a long and complicated story, from which it is only too obvious that the father of the future Chief Baron had been the victim of a cruel injustice. This was the removal of his name from the rolls in 1842, by the Irish Lord Chancellor, Sir Edward Sugden, afterwards Lord St. Leonards.

Sugden had, it appears, struck Palles off the rolls of his court in connection with his alleged conduct towards a client, one Captain Goold, on the allegation that he had joined in the forgery of a deed in order to charge certain of Goold's property. Goold's father owned extensive estates in Tipperary and Cork, which he had incumbered. These estates were subject to the elder Goold's marriage settlement. A question arose as to whether he held them as tenant for life or in tail, and since the views of learned counsel differed on this thorny point of real property law, a suit was instituted in Chancery. At this stage, Captain Goold returned from India and sought to enter into a deed of re-settlement with his father.

Andrew Palles sent the papers in the case to one James Joseph Hardy, a member of the Bar, who acted for both of the Goolds. Hardy, who was one of the founders of the first Irish law school, the Dublin Law Institute, was then in an extensive business as a conveyancing counsel, and the petition states that he was in the habit of " taking instructions by personal communication with his clients." He drew the deed of re-settlement with immoderate haste, and he appointed Palles and himself as trustees. Shortly afterwards Captain Goold decided to marry, and the papers were again sent to Hardy to draw his marriage settlement. Hardy discovered a flaw in the first deed and, realising that this would imperil his professional reputation, he adopted the extraordinary expedient of forging a complete set of deeds in order to put matters to rights. Of this Andrew Palles was, of course, completely ignorant.

Captain Goold soon found himself in financial difficulties, and Andrew Palles advanced and raised, on his own account, large sums of money in order to stave off proceedings against Goold. The creditors pressed the latter and, through him, the hapless Palles. In September, 1842, Palles was attached at the suit of one of the creditors and committed to prison in the Dublin Marshalsea. While he was in prison the suit which was pending in Chancery resulted in the business of the forged deeds being revealed. The Lord Chancellor, without hearing Palles in his defence, peremptorily struck him off the rolls, and ordered the case of the real author of his misfortune, Hardy, to be investigated by the Benchers of King's Inns. Of the latter's fate, history is silent, and it is difficult to regard him with any sympathy.

These disasters had their immediate effect on the Palles family. The fine house in Mountjoy Square was let off, and the family moved to a smaller house at No. 26, Upper Temple Street. On his release from prison, Andrew Palles withdrew to London. He did not petition Sugden while the latter retained the Irish seals, presumably because he felt that there was little purpose in so doing. With the fall of Peel's government in 1846, however, the advent of the administration of Lord John Russell brought a new Lord Chancellor, Maziere Brady, and it was to him that Palles directed his plea for vindication of his character.

Brady referred the whole matter to two of the Masters in Chancery, Edward Litton and Jeremiah Murphy, and on 9th July, 1847, they were able to report that in their considered opinion, Palles had been blameless from the first, and they recommended that he be restored to the rolls. This the Lord Chancellor did without delay.

It is pleasant to be able to record that Maziere Brady lived long enough to see the son of Andrew Palles at the head of his profession and on the threshold of the rank of Solicitor-General, and that in 1874, Christopher Palles succeeded to the chief place in the Court of Exchequer which Brady had occupied thirty years earlier.

Andrew Palles felt, as he was entitled to feel, a certain

pride in his tardy vindication, and the copy of the petition in the Clongowes library bears the endorsement, in his own handwriting: "My dear sir, I am sure the enclosed will gratify you." The Jesuits, indeed, never lost faith in Palles, whose politics and religion may well have made him the victim of the party spleen of the future Lord St. Leonards. There is extant a letter, written from London on 8th October, 1844, and addressed to the Rector of the school, in which Andrew said that he had heard from his wife that the Society of Jesus wished to abate the pensions of the two boys because of his straitened circumstances. He thanked the Rector for his help, but refused the kindly offer, stating that he was making good progress towards a reduction of his liabilities. Earlier, in May, 1844, he had written from Upper Temple Street, enclosing the half-yearly fees to the school, and saying that things were becoming more hopeful with him. He added: "I am free to declare, that there is no money I have found for years for which I have got so much value, as that paid into your establishment." In later years, when the Chief Baron was in a position to do so, he did not forget the kindness of the Clongowes fathers shown to him and his family in time of need.

All things considered, it is more than likely that the protracted family crisis extending over almost the whole of Christopher's school career resulted in his premature withdrawal from Clongowes. In any event, he left school in the summer of 1847 and he entered Trinity College, Dublin in the autumn of that year.

III

TRINITY COLLEGE

CHRISTOPHER PALLES was entered as a pensioner on the books of Trinity College, Dublin, on 23rd November, 1847. His tutor was William Lee, later Professor of Ecclesiastical History and Archdeacon of Dublin. The fact that he had not yet attained his sixteenth year would not have been a matter for comment in the College at that time. In the eighteenth century the average age at which boys came up to College had been about fifteen, and though this steadily rose after the Union, a certain degree of immaturity was still not regarded as being unusual. In addition, the fact that young Palles lived under parental supervision may have influenced the decision for an early matriculation, though as has already been suggested, economic pressures were probably decisive in this respect.

In the autumn of 1847 Ireland was slowly recovering from the catastrophic famine of the previous season. The good harvest of that year was a blessing, it is true; but the death of O'Connell in May must have been regarded as the end of all hope by those who sympathized with his aims. The disturbances of the next year lay ahead and 1848, the year of revolution, had, as yet, no significance for the Irish people.

From the point of view of a newcomer to the life of a university, probably the most popular topic of discussion was that of the reform of higher education in Ireland, and in the light of Palles's later views, it will be convenient to say something here of the place of Trinity College in this controversy.

Before 1793 the University of Dublin was closed to all but members of the Established Church. A provision in the Relief Act of that year enabled Catholics to enter and graduate at the university, though the fellowships, scholarships and professorships were still restricted to those who conformed to the establishment. The Act of 1793, it should be remembered, also provided that if any future college were to be founded within the university, it should be free from all religious tests. At the present day, indeed, it is often conveniently forgotten that many middle-class Catholics availed themselves of the 1793 relaxation, and up to 1845 they appear to have entered the College without any overt ecclesiastical disapproval. The fact that Palles himself was enabled to enjoy the benefits of the College at all was indicative of the prevailing position. Nevertheless, the situation could not be regarded as being in any way satisfactory for the majority of Irishmen, and an event which occurred shortly before Palles went up served to emphasise this.

In 1843, Denis Caulfield Heron, a Catholic student who was later to attain eminence at the Bar and to become a Serjeant-at-Law—he was elected a Bencher of King's Inns on the same day as Palles—entered for the foundation scholarship competition, and on the results of his answering was entitled to be elected. He refused to make the mandatory declaration against transubstantiation, however, and so did not obtain a scholarship. Heron called for a visitation against the decision of the Board of the College, but his appeal was dismissed on the ground that the Act of 1793 did not permit Catholics or Protestant Dissenters to become members of the corporation of the College. He later published a book in which he set out his claims to be admitted, maintaining that this exclusive attitude was illegal. The Catholic laity were extremely dissatisfied with the decision, and it seems that the government under Peel were stimulated by it to take action.

The spokesman of the Catholic claims, Sir Thomas Wyse, put forward a comprehensive scheme for a national system of Irish education at every level. He was a believer in mixed education, the education of Catholics and Protestants in the same institutions, with combined secular and divided religious instruction. This, as has been seen, was the plan operated in the "National" primary schools, of which Wyse was the advocate. Mixed education was supported by some of the Catholic bishops, though it was opposed by a clamorous majority of them; and this opposition was shared by the Presbyterians of Ulster.

Peel felt that a policy of conciliation in the matter of education might divert the Irish Catholics from the more pressing claims of Repeal and, in 1845, two measures were introduced with this object in view. The first provided a capital grant for Maynooth College and increased its annual revenues. This had the dual effect of placating episcopal opinion to some extent, and also of removing the seminary from the university controversy. The second measure aimed at setting up a number of undenominational colleges for the laity in the provinces, and this gave rise to a dispute of extraordinary bitterness.

The plan did not involve any interference with the status of Trinity College, for the suggestion that Catholics might be made eligible for all the emoluments of that foundation resulted in an outcry from the extreme evangelical party. Instead, three Queen's Colleges, at Belfast, Cork and Galway, were to be set up, free from religious tests, to cater for the needs of those who felt themselves excluded from Trinity. Popular opinion on the merits of these new colleges was sharply divided, O'Connell condemning them as " Godless," and the Young Irelanders welcoming them as a means of implementing the teachings of Thomas Davis. A similar cleavage was apparent amongst the Catholic bishops, who sought concessions from Peel in the matter of providing Catholic professors of history, logic, metaphysics, moral philosophy, geology and anatomy for students of that persuasion, and also of providing that a proportion of the academic staff should be Catholics. These points Peel refused to concede and, after a protracted inter-episcopal wrangle, the Papacy condemned the new colleges. The Irish hierarchy endorsed this anathema, and went ahead with their own plans for the foundation of a Catholic University.

In the meantime, the Trinity authorities were startled into removing some of the anomalies in their own constitution. In 1851 a Royal Commission was appointed to enquire into the state and discipline of the University of Dublin, and as a result of their deliberations the College set up non-foundation scholarships for those who could not subscribe to the religious tests. Many of these were won by men who afterwards distinguished themselves in the public life of the country and abroad. The first scholar elected, Thomas Maguire, was afterwards a Fellow. John Naish was a future Lord Chancellor of Ireland, while John Casey became professor of mathematics in the Catholic University.

Giving evidence before the Royal Commission on the College, in 1906, Lord Justice FitzGibbon dealt with the allegation that Trinity was resorted to by " a mere handful of Catholics " who saw in it " the only road to professional advancement and social recognition." He pointed out that there is nothing denominational in the attractiveness of any such road :

> " These are the fruits and rewards of higher education, and the record of the successes of this ' mere handful of Catholics ' is the conclusive proof of the excellence of their education, and of their fitness to receive it."

FitzGibbon added, by way of a tribute to Palles :

> " Clongowes College is the largest and best equipped residential school in Ireland, and its teaching staff is second to none, as a community of scholarly gentlemen, unless it be so to the Fellows and Professors of Trinity College; the roll of the Clongowes Union, of which the Lord Chief Baron is the President, is an index of the work done by Trinity College for the pupils of a single school, for Clongowes has sent many of its most distinguished pupils to Trinity College, and they have, in large numbers, made their way to eminence."

Apart from these external events, the period immediately before Palles' entry into the College was one of radical internal reform in matters of education. Dr. Bartholomew Lloyd, who had been Professor of Mathematics from 1813 to 1822, succeeded to the Chair of Natural and Experi-

mental Philosophy in the latter year, and became Provost
of the College in 1831. During the time he taught mathematics he effected a complete revolution in its study. By
his lectures and his writings he introduced the students
under his direction to modern analytic methods then in
vogue on the continent of Europe, and his researches in
the field of applied mathematics did much to stimulate
interest in that branch of the science. The fact that these
reforms were effected in the period immediately before the
arrival of Palles was a fortunate one; for he became a
member of the school of mathematics at a time
when it was staffed by those who made the name of
the Dublin school famous throughout the world of scholarship. When Lloyd died in 1837, moreover, he was succeeded as Provost by another mathematician, Franc
Sadleir, whose tenure of office spanned Palles' undergraduate career.

The choice of subject was a wise one for Palles. Sir
William Rowan Hamilton, Ireland's greatest mathematician, was then at the height of his powers, though his
work was rivalled by that of John Hewitt Jellett and
George Salmon, both of whom lived to rule the College.
Jellett's work on the calculus of variations and the theory
of friction acquired for him great distinction, while in later
years Salmon, who had been awarded the Copley Medal
of the Royal Society, forsook mathematics for the realm
of theological controversy. Provided with such a stimulus,
it is not a matter of surprise that Palles made good
progress with his undergraduate studies. Among his contemporaries were men of the calibre of Thomas Kingsmill
Abbott, whose work on Aristotelian logic has been familiar
to generations of Trinity men; John Robert Leslie, later
Professor of Experimental Philosophy; Samuel Walker, a
future Lord Chancellor; and William Drennan Andrews, a
future puisne Baron of the Exchequer.

The younger members of the academic staff included
John Kells Ingram, whose: *Who Fears to Speak of '98?*
has achieved immortality; Joseph Galbraith, a founder of
the Home Government Association, who coined the phrase

"Home Rule"; and Samuel Haughton, whose achievements as an applied mathematician gained widespread application, if little publicity, in his invention of the "long drop" method of judicial hanging. In the words of a contemporary College song:

> "Joe Galbraith, though Republican,
> Knows how to *Rule at Home*,
> A Garibaldian abroad,
> A very Pope at home.
> Sam Haughton is a wily man,
> Of scientific scope,
> And yet we know he'd *hang* himself
> If he but got the *rope*."

Remarkable too was the redoubtable Joseph Carson, Fellow from 1837 to 1898. A stern upholder of the older methods of examining, Carson demanded an accurate and detailed knowledge of the prescribed books, a trait which is illustrated by the question he once put to a candidate being examined in Old Testament divinity: "How many knives did the Jews bring up out of captivity?" (*Ezra I. 9*). The unhappy candidate did not know. "You don't know," said Carson. "You're going out to teach your flock, and you don't know how many knives the Jews brought up out of captivity!"

The revival of the College Historical Society within the College in 1843, under the Auditorship of William Connor Magee (later Archbishop of York), brought to the forefront men such as Edward Sullivan, afterwards Master of the Rolls, Michael Morris, later Lord Chief Justice, and others with whom Palles was to have a close connection in his professional life. He himself does not seem to have taken a very active part in the affairs of the Society, though he was a member of the old Philosophical Society in 1848-1849. It is possible that he found little time to spare from his mathematical reading. In addition, he had already chosen a professional career, for in Trinity Term, 1849, he was admitted a student of King's Inns.

In after life Palles always spoke with affection of his old College, to which he felt he owed so much. Later, we shall see that his views on higher education for the Irish majority were coloured to a great extent by his experiences at Trinity. Giving evidence before the Robertson Commission in 1901, he stated with characteristic vehemence that his religious beliefs were entirely unassailed during his sojourn there.

> "Occasionally," he said, "I had an argument with one of my fellow students upon questions of religion. In the interval between mathematical discussions they sometimes used to turn to theology, and I may say there was nothing that ever did me so much good because when I found various points discussed, some of which I had never heard before, I found it my duty to read the Catholic doctrine upon these subjects."

Here one perceives an emphatic rejection of the "hot house" theory of sectarian education which then prevailed in episcopal circles and which ultimately frustrated the true solution of the Irish university question in 1908. His pride in his connection with a great centre of learning enabled him to see beyond the more circumscribed approach to the problem, and to perceive merits in a system which was afterwards condemned by some of his co-religionists.

Assiduous reading had its reward. At the examinations held in 1851, Palles was awarded a Senior Moderatorship in Mathematics, being placed fourth in order of merit. It is idle to speculate that if the Fellowships had then been open to Catholics—a step not taken until 1873—the course of his future life might have been entirely different. His scholarly ability would have inclined him towards academic pursuits, and a Fellowship of the College would have been a great prize. The premature death of his classfellow, John Robert Leslie, in 1881, would have placed in his grasp the Chair of Experimental Philosophy. The gain of the Dublin school of mathematics would have been the irreparable loss of the common law world. But it happened otherwise, for Christopher Palles had already embarked on his chosen career.

28 CHRISTOPHER PALLES

IV

A STUDENT OF THE LAW

IT has already been said that a modern visitor to the Four
Courts will see little change in the externals of the building, for despite the ravages of time and of revolution, it
presents much the same appearance as it did when
Christopher Palles was called to the Bar. The same can be
said of James Gandon's other masterpiece, King's Inns.
When Palles became a law student in 1849 this building
was less than fifty years old, being completed in 1816-17.
It is an excellent example of the architect's genius and it
has survived largely intact though as one writer has
shrewdly observed, much of Gandon's best work in Dublin
has been " bombarded, burnt, rebuilt or at best added to."

Much has happened to change the structure of the Irish
legal system in the past century, however, and in order to
appreciate the sort of society which Palles joined as a
student in 1849, it becomes necessary to say something
about the courts and the legal profession as they existed
at that time.

As legal readers will appreciate, the present system of
courts in the Republic of Ireland is a later modification of
the pattern set in 1877, when a fusion was effected of the
earlier tribunals into one Supreme Court, preserving in its
several divisions the jurisdictions exercised by its predecessors. The modification, indeed, has been slight, and
the Supreme Court (set up for the Irish Free State in 1924)
corresponds almost exactly to its forerunner, the Court of
Appeal, under the 1877 reforms, while a High Court (its
divisions abolished but the dichotomy of its work retained)
still does service for the Court it replaced. In Northern
Ireland, moreover, the 1877 plan is still in substantial
operation.

In 1849 the system was radically different. The common

law was administered in four distinct tribunals—the Four
Courts that gave their names to the building—each having
its own hierarchy of judges, and each dealing with a different aspect of the legal system. First, there were three
common law courts, the Queen's Bench, the Common
Pleas, and the Exchequer. The first two were presided over
by Chief Justices, while the Exchequer was headed by a
Lord Chief Baron. Secondly, there was the Court of
Chancery, with the Lord Chancellor at its head and the
Master of the Rolls as his assistant. In addition to these
four courts, there were two other courts of special jurisdiction, the Court of Admiralty and the Prerogative Court—
an ecclesiastical tribunal with jurisdiction in probate
matters. Each of the common law courts had three puisne
judges, and these with the others comprised sixteen judges
in all. From the common law courts an appeal lay to the
Court of Exchequer Chamber, composed of the judges of
all three courts, with an ultimate appeal to the House of
Lords. Appeals from the Court of Chancery went directly
to the Lords, though shortly after Palles was called to the
Bar an intermediate Court of Appeal in Chancery was set
up.

This complicated scheme had remained unaltered in
Ireland for centuries. The original " Four Courts " dated
from medieval times, the Court of Prerogative from the
seventeenth century, and the Court of Admiralty from 1784.
The latter had the doubtful distinction of having as one of
its judges the only judicial personage ever removed for
corruption, Sir Jonah Barrington. Since the time of
Grattan's parliament all the judges of the superior courts
had held office during good behaviour and could only be
removed by the Crown on an address of both Houses of
Parliament. Before the Union the Lord Chancellor had
presided in the Irish House of Lords, and, even after the
Irish legislature was abolished, the practice was continued
of his vacating his seat on a change of Government. Up to
the appointment of Maziere Brady in 1846, the Great
Seal of Ireland was the perquisite of English lawyers.

It remains to say something of the incumbents of the

several judicial offices at the time Palles went to the Bar. Brady, the Lord Chancellor, had been Lord Chief Baron in 1840, Chancellor under Russell from 1846 to 1852, and had returned to office in the same year, under Aberdeen. He had risen to prominence after 1832, under Liberal Governments, and he first attracted attention as a member of the commission on Irish municipal corporations. He had a common law training, and though he spent almost twenty years as head of the Chancery, he was never a master of equity. His judgments are not distinguished for their learning, but he did possess the great merit of being able to extract what he believed to be the relevant principle from a mass of detail. Taking office again, under Palmerston in 1859, he held the seals until 1866. Brady was created a baronet in 1869 and died two years later, leaving as his successor to the family honours a son, Sir Francis Brady, who was familiar to a later generation of lawyers as an amiable if antique Chairman of Quarter Sessions.

The Master of the Rolls, T. B. Cusack Smith, was a man of different stamp. As Attorney-General at the State Trials, in 1844, his quick temper had impelled him to challenge one of the defendants' counsel, Gerald FitzGibbon, to a duel; and when he attained the Bench in 1846 this hasty disposition did not desert him. Smith had the distinction of being the third member of his family to become a judge in Ireland, his father having been a Baron of the Exchequer and his grandfather Master of the Rolls.

In 1849, the Chief Justices of the Queen's Bench and the Common Pleas were Francis Blackburne and John Doherty. They were soon to be succeeded by two men, whose reputations assured for them a lasting place in Irish legal annals. The septuagenarian Thomas Langlois Lefroy, who went to the Queen's Bench in 1850, had been a puisne judge since 1841, and he lived to preside in his ninety-first year. In 1856, a debate was initiated in the House of Commons on the allegation that half the Irish judges were incapacitated by illness or age, and the House witnessed the extraordinary spectacle of Lefroy being defended by his son. Ten years later a similar agitation was equally inconclusive, notwithstanding the fact that it was then stated (with more humour than truth) that his son, Anthony Lefroy, had already applied for exemption from service on committees in the Commons on the ground of advancing years. The Chief Justice was able to show that he had not failed to act as a judge of Assize in the space of twenty-five years, though the issue had been raised because he had exhibited such extreme physical feebleness when trying a murder case at King's County assizes that Lawson, the Attorney-General, was compelled to place before him the curial part of the death sentence, written in a large hand, and actually stood beside him on the Bench, while the aged judge repeated word after word.

James Monahan presided in the Common Pleas. He was one of the distinguished Catholics to whom the Relief Act had opened up a legal career. He rose to eminence in the Chancery under Sugden, and he led the Connaught Circuit for many years. Monahan tended to be impulsive and, as a contemporary put it, " he seasoned his conversation with oaths, like Wellington." He used to tell a story against himself concerning an appeal in which he was engaged before the House of Lords. His leaders were Bethell (later Lord Westbury) and Sir George Turner. At the consultation before the hearing, Bethell disdained authority, but Monahan harried him with precedents. After a time, Bethell observed, " Turner, that voluble Irish savage, really knows a little law."

The Exchequer was ruled by the man whom Palles was to succeed in office, David Richard Pigot, Lord Chief Baron for twenty-eight years. Pigot had started life as a physician, but was later called to the Bar and went the Munster Circuit. A liberal in politics, he was a Law Officer before attaining the Bench. He was a most scrupulous and conscientious judge and this merit, indeed, became a failing, for he devoted too much time to the *minutiae* of litigation. His judgments, nevertheless, display legal ability of a high order, and even today, it is a valuable asset to have Pigot on one's side.

As is to be expected, the Bar of Ireland, in common with

the other learned professions, has always reflected the
national fortunes of the day. During the greater part of
the eighteenth century, therefore, the Bar represented the
exclusive nature of Irish society. The Bench was staffed
by Englishmen. The operation of the Penal Laws prevented
Irish Catholics from entering the legal profession; and this
exclusiveness had the inevitable effect of degrading it.
Paradoxically enough, the very complexity of the penal
code itself redounded to the benefit of the Bar, for its laby-
rinthine intricacy produced a spate of litigation. As a
result, men like Tisdall, Singleton, Marley, Bowes and
the great Anthony Malone came to the forefront of the
profession and established standards of taste which were
to endure. Fees were high, the houses of the leading
lawyers were nearly always in the finest style, and Dublin
society revolved around the more fashionable members
of the Bar.

The constitutional revolution of 1782 and the admission
of Catholics to the Bar in 1793 had a most stimulating
effect on the profession. The increased authority of the
Irish Parliament and the number of its constituencies made
it a lucrative field for lawyers. Hussey Burgh, Yelverton,
FitzGibbon, Ponsonby and Curran brought their genius to
College Green; and the debates on the Union produced
Plunket, Saurin, Bushe and O'Connell. Even the passing of
the Act of Union itself produced in its opponents some
of the finest figures in the history of the Irish Bar. This
is not the place to write of the merits of O'Connell, the
politician. O'Connell the advocate, however, was probably
unique in the annals of any Bar. Emancipation restored
the equilibrium of the Bar and its tardy recognition in
the sphere of judicial preferment, commencing with the
elevation of O'Loghlen, was the beginning of the golden
era of Irish legal history. The divisions of race and of creed
were all but forgotten within the walls of the Four Courts;
and a true union of hearts was developed between the
members of the Bar which has never been destroyed. At
times the bitterness of party feeling may have sundered

them, but the fellowship of the Bar of Ireland has always been proof against lasting discord.

Christopher Palles embarked on the study of law at a time when the whole subject of legal education in Ireland was under review. The Honourable Society of King's Inns, the voluntary association of barristers regulating admission to their number, had been formed in 1607. It succeeded an earlier body, said to have been founded in the reign of Edward I, and by the end of the eighteenth century membership was open to all judges, barristers, attorneys and solicitors.

It is extremely doubtful whether the Society in Dublin ever provided any form of teaching for its students prior to 1850. The elaborate instruction by the Reader, the " bolts " and " moots " of the London Inns of Court, which had formed the staple of the education of the Elizabethan law student, had not lapsed in Ireland; they had never come into existence. The requirement of keeping terms in London, imposed on Irish law students in 1542—a rule which was not relaxed until 1885—may have had something to do with this absence of any provision for instruction, though it is to be feared that there were other and baser motives, for an attempt to found a Dublin Law Institute in 1839 was frustrated by lack of professional enthusiasm and financial support from the Benchers of King's Inns.

In the University of Dublin there had been provision for the granting of degrees in law from the foundation. The charter of Elizabeth I, under which the College was founded, conferred the privilege, and the seventeenth century College statutes refer to a Professor of Jurisprudence. The acquisition of a degree in law was probably a frequent occurrence, for although no equivalent of " Doctors' Commons " ever existed in Ireland, the degree of Doctor in Laws was always required by candidates for admission to the rank of advocate in the Prerogative and

Admiralty Courts. Evidence given before the Royal Commission on Trinity College in 1853 indicates that the exercises for the degree were " mere forms ". There had been a Regius Professorship of Feudal and English Law since 1761, and its first occupant, Francis Staughton Sullivan, made some contribution to legal learning. His successors, however, were very much part-time holders of the Chair. Patrick Duigenan, for instance, was a practising barrister and, in addition, was Judge of the Prerogative Court, Vicar-General of the dioceses of Armagh, Meath and Elphin, King's Advocate-General and a member of Parliament for Armagh. Mountifort Longfield, better known as an economist, combined the duties of the Chair with the office of Judge of the Landed Estates Court.

In 1848 certain reforms were carried out, and the new arrangements came into effect just as Palles became a student at King's Inns. An agreement with the University was concluded, whereby all candidates for call to the Bar were required to attend two years' College lectures. In addition, two new Professorships were founded at King's Inns, and attendance at their lectures was made obligatory. The formal exercises for the University degrees in law were still retained. In 1858, a change was made, and it became possible to proceed to the degree of Bachelor in Laws, either by two years' study in the College, by passing an examination, or by purchase, after six years' practice at the Bar. Palles seems to have adopted the latter course, for he proceeded LL.B. in 1860 and LL.D. in the same year. He, thus, possessed the curious distinction of having a double doctorate, for his old University conferred upon him the degree of LL.D. *honoris causa* in 1914.

To comply with the statute of Henry VIII, Palles was admitted at Gray's Inn on 15th January, 1851, and he duly kept his terms there in the prescribed manner. In those days, most of the Irish students went to Gray's, and it was not until later that the Middle Temple became popular with them, owing possibly to the fact that Edward Carson was a member. Lincoln's Inn had always been suspect by Irishmen, a feeling that seems to have been mutual, for in its *Black Book* it is recorded that in the early days of the Inn, the Irish were relegated to the dovecote.

One can imagine that for the youthful Palles, life in early Victorian London was a source of wonderment, not unmixed with awe. In old age he delighted to recount to the younger members of the Bar on circuit—" his young friends," as he called them—the tale of his first journey to London to keep term. His mother had been warned of the dangers besetting a traveller in the great city, and carefully sewed up fifteen golden pounds in the lining of Christopher's waistcoat. His efforts to extricate this hidden wealth were recalled by the Chief Baron in terms that brought a smile to his face and captivated his listeners.

Palles appears to have read law with the same care as he pursued the study of mathematics. As one of the first students in Ireland ever tested by examination, he satisfied the Benchers that he possessed an adequate knowledge of the principles of the common law to be allowed to practise it, and in Hilary Term, 1853, he was called to the Bar of Ireland by the Lord Chancellor, Maziere Brady.

V

THE HOME CIRCUIT

At the time that Christopher Palles was called to the Bar, the fortunes of his family seem to have undergone a change for the better, and the house at Number 26, Upper Temple Street had been exchanged for a more imposing one, Number 53, Summerhill. The eldest son, Andrew, had obtained the diploma of the school of engineering at Trinity College, and had proceeded B.A. in the following year. In common with many young professional men of his generation, he lost no time in emigrating to the New World, where he settled in Kingston, Ontario. In 1853 he married a widow, Jane Hawke, and by her had four children. The eldest, a boy, Andrew Christopher, was killed in the South African war, and the surviving relatives of the Chief Baron are descended from his daughters. After working in Philadelphia and in India, Andrew returned to Ireland about 1871, and when Christopher became Lord Chief Baron, he appointed his brother as his registrar, a position which he occupied until his death in 1900.

In 1853 the road to success at the Irish Bar was not unlike that followed today. The newly-called barrister joined one of the circuits and won renown, if he could, in the work on assize before migrating to the more remunerative field of a Dublin practice. This circuit system, as it was known in those days, has been swept away; and, it is thought, a word on its operation may not be out of place.

Although itinerant justices were traversing Ireland on commissions of " oyer and terminer " and " gaol delivery " as early as the thirteenth century, it was not until the reign of James I that the circuit system was formally established. As early as 1570, indeed, assizes were being held in the counties of Dublin, Kildare, Carlow, Kilkenny, Louth, Meath, Westmeath, Longford, and the King's County, and by 1610, assizes covered every part of the country. In the summer of 1614 there appeared mapped out for the judges five circuits, embracing the whole island and bearing the names familiar to everyone acquainted with the Irish legal system down to 1921—the Connaught, the Leinster, the Munster, the North-West and the North-East.. At first, only part of the country was travelled in the Spring Assize, but in 1617 the same circuits were assigned as in the summer, and for over a hundred and fifty years this system continued to operate.

In the spring of 1796 a change was made by Lord Clare. A new arrangement was announced in which an extra circuit, to be called the Home Circuit, was established, comprising the six counties adjoining Dublin— Meath, Westmeath, Carlow, Kildare, the King's and the Queen's. The Home Circuit lasted just short of ninety years, being abolished in a further re-organisation of 1885. It has been alleged by one writer that during the time of its existence, " infirm and senior judges found refuge upon it," because of its proximity to the capital, but this nearness to the Four Courts had its advantages, for it attracted to the circuit rising men in practice. In addition, the Chiefs of the various courts were stimulated to travel on a circuit which did not take them further afield than Carlow or Mullingar, and so its judicial standards were actually enhanced. This was the circuit joined by Christopher Palles when, at a meeting of the Home Bar, held on 6th March, 1854, at Tullamore, he was proposed by George Battersby, Q.C., and duly elected.

Under the circuit system operative down to the 1921 settlement, the assize courts in Ireland had full jurisdiction to deal with every department of the administration of justice at first instance. All indictable crime of a serious nature was tried at assize, and the court was also competent to hear civil actions commenced by writ, though the growth of the Quarter Sessions under the chairmanship of the Assistant-Barristers (later the County Court judges) deprived the assizes of much original jurisdiction on the civil side. Originally, indeed, procedure by " English

bill " instead of by writ (a simplified method of commencing a suit) was an Irish invention to give the assize judges
additional jurisdiction. This "civil bill" jurisdiction, as it
was called, was transferred to the Assistant-Barristers in
1796 and, thereafter, much of the civil work of the assizes
consisted in hearing appeals from the Assistant-Barristers
and their successors, the County Court judges.

One of the results of the structural changes made in the
judicial system in 1924 was to rob the administration of
justice of much of its ceremonial. The time is fast
approaching when few, if any, in the southern part of the
country will remember the pageantry and dignity of an
assize, and it may be of interest to describe the business of
opening an assize, as it must have appeared to Palles when
he became a law student. It was a scene which he was to
witness on countless occasions over the next sixty-three
years, yet from that first occasion it must have remained
with him as an indelible memory.

Before leaving Dublin for their progress around the
circuit, the judges signed a series of precepts to the Sheriffs
of each county, calling on them, inter alia, to summon
jurors to try all such matters as might come before them.
The authority to hold an assize was derived from the
Queen's Commission given to the judges, and the main
business of opening the assize involved the reading of this
commission.

When the judges arrived in the assize town and went
straight to Court, they did so robed, having been met at
the railway station, or the outskirts of the town, by the
Sheriff with an escort. The judge who was to try crime—
"the Judge in Commission"—wore scarlet robes trimmed
with ermine and full-bottomed wig. The other judge wore
black robes trimmed with ermine, and a bob-wig, and
carried his three-corner hat, or "tricorne". At the court-
house, the judge in commission was conducted to the
Crown Court by the Sheriff, while the other judge was
taken to his room by the Under-Sheriff. On entering the
Crown Court, the judge in commission stood at his desk,
on which his three-cornered hat had been placed. His crier

then made two proclamations: "All persons having anything to do before my Lords, the Queen's Justices of
Assize, Oyer and Terminer, and General Gaol Delivery for
this County of——, draw near and give your attendance;"
and "My Lords, the Queen's Justices, do strictly charge
and command all persons to keep silence whilst the Commission of our Sovereign Lady the Queen is produced and
read." The Clerk of the Crown then read a condensed
version of the commission. When he reached the passage
which included the phrase " Our Judges for the time being
o f our Courts of . . . .," the Clerk of the Crown substituted
the name of the judge who was standing above him, and
turned and bowed to him. The judge in return raised his
three-cornered hat to his head, bowed, and replaced it on
his desk.

When the commission had been read, the judge's crier
said " God Save the Queen!" and the judge then took his
seat. A message was then sent to the other judge, who had
been waiting in his room, that the commission had been
opened, and he then went into his court to start the civil
work. The crier in the Crown Court then said " Mr. High
Sheriff of this County, be pleased to return the several precepts and writs to you directed and delivered or returnable
here this day that my Lords the Queen's Justices may proceed thereon." The Sheriff then handed to the judge a roll
of papers tied up with tape. The judge received them with
a bow, and handed them to the Clerk of the Crown.

There followed the swearing of the Grand Jury. The
crier said " Gentlemen of the Grand Jury, be pleased to
answer your names and save your fines." The Clerk of the
Crown then read out twenty-three names, and each in
turn said " Here." The oath was administered to each by
the judge's registrar, and there then came an admonition
from the crier " My Lords the Queen's Justices do strictly
charge and command all persons to keep silence whilst the
charge is given to this Grand Jury upon pain of fine and
imprisonment." The judge then addressed the Grand
Jury on the " state of the county," the members of the
Bar, by custom, being absent. Although the address was

intended to deal with the business in hand, some judges used the occasion to unburden themselves of their views on the state of the country at large. Thus, Mr. Justice Fletcher, of the Court of Common Pleas, delivered a fiery political charge to the Grand Jury at Wexford in 1814, and Baron Smith was accused by O'Connell of replying from the Bench to speeches in Parliament. He was also charged by O'Connell with trying prisoners at night!

When the charge was over, the Grand Jury retired to their room, and the judge retired to his, where he put off his full-bottomed wig and replaced it with his bob-wig. He waited until the Grand Jury were ready with a " true Bill " of indictment. When they returned with an indictment, indorsed " true Bill " or otherwise, it had to be handed direct by the foreman to the Clerk of the Crown. The judge in commission then began trying prisoners.

In earlier and unhappier times, the judges' work on assize must have been beyond endurance. A hundred and twenty persons awaited trial at the Spring Assizes at Dundalk in 1793. In 1797, the Summer Assizes at Armagh heard a hundred and fifty-one indictments, and the judge had what a contemporary newspaper called " the Awful and Unexampled Duty " of pronouncing the sentence of death on twenty men together. By 1853, however, the country was in a more tranquil state. The disturbances of 1848 were behind, and those of the late 1860s lay ahead.

When Palles joined the Home Circuit, the number of members was not very large and, as a result, a strong spirit of friendship existed between them. Walter Hussey Griffith was the Father, having been called to the bar in 1817, and the leaders were Abraham Brewster, Q.C., Francis Macdonagh, Q.C., George Battersby, Q.C., Hamilton Smyth, Q.C., Edmund Hayes, Q.C., and Walter Berwick, Q.C. Macdonagh probably led the circuit. He has been described as a " dexterous advocate," but he seems to have been disliked by his brethren, it being thought that his air of self-esteem savoured of a lack of sincerity. He had defended O'Connell at the State Trials and in 1853 he was at the head of his profession. He survived, indeed, to take part in the trials of Parnell and his associates in 1881. It was not long before he encountered the youthful Palles. In a case before Chief Justice Lefroy, Palles applied for a non-suit in an ejectment on grounds of extreme technicality. He was opposed by Macdonagh, whose knowledge of law was said to be slight, and the latter kept on decrying " his learned young friend." Palles won his point before the venerable Chief Justice, who that evening was heard to remark, " Horace for once is wrong, ' proximos illi *non* occupavit Palles honores '." Macdonagh and Palles were to meet again, when the latter was a Law Officer of the Crown, in the sensational Newtown-Stewart murder trial.

Many years, later, Palles was to recount to Tim Healy that, when he was a junior to Macdonagh in a chancery suit, the latter added a plea which was successfully demurred to by the other side. Palles had himself opposed the insertion of the plea. After judgment against them, Macdonagh turned to his junior, saying, " Young man, I hope this will teach you to be more careful in future!"

George Battersby succeeded Griffith as Father of the Home, and later became an ecclesiastical judge. He was an advocate with an independent cast of mind, and, on one occasion, he crossed swords with Lefroy. The Chief Justice told him in a peremptory manner to sit down. The same evening a resolution was unanimously passed by the members of the circuit, binding its members not to appear in court before Lefroy unless he apologised to Battersby. The next morning he made an ample apology.

Of the others, Hayes became a Queen's Bench judge; Berwick succeeded to the Court of Bankruptcy and lost his life on the Irish Mail in the Abergale disaster of 1868; and Abraham Brewster became Attorney-General in the year of Palles's call. He was later a Lord Justice of Appeal and Lord Chancellor.

Mention must also be made of two men who had a decisive influence on the course of modern Irish law, John Thomas Ball and Samuel Walker. Ball had been called in 1840, and soon became an experienced advocate in the ecclesiastical courts. Later, he made his name in the common law, ultimately becoming Lord Chancellor. His political career in the interim is not without interest. In 1868, he stood for Dublin University as a Radical, but three years later he gained a seat, as the Conservative Attorney-General. His variety of political principles was the subject of a sally made at his expense by Richard Dowse, when Attorney-General. At question time in the Commons, Ball pressed Dowse to give the exact date of some incident. Dowse said : —

"I cannot give the right hon. gentlemen the exact date, but I will give him the best approximation I can. It was between the time he contested Trinity College as a Radical and was defeated, and the time when he contested Trinity College as a Tory and was elected."

Walker was a little junior to Palles at the Bar, and he lived to hold the great seal of Ireland. He first entered the House of Commons, in 1884, as a Solicitor-General for Ireland. Sitting on the Treasury bench as a parliamentary novice, he was asked what he thought of his first debate.

"Well," he said, "I could hardly believe my senses, as I heard men on either side making the most material statements without even a scrap of an affidavit to support them."

According to tradition, the first brief ever held by Palles was at Mullingar Assizes, when he was called upon to defend a prisoner. He delivered an eloquent and impassioned address on behalf of the innocent in the dock, it is said, and was warmly congratulated by his brethren. A voice from the public gallery expressed sympathetic agreement with the orator by a shout of "Bravo, gossoon!" though, alas, the annals are silent as to the fate of the prisoner.

The work on the Home Circuit was very heavy, and it was not long before Palles was getting his share of it. For the county Kildare, the assizes sat alternately in Athy and

Naas, and as Naas was usually the last town of the circuit, the proceedings concluded there with some jollification. Much of the prosperity of the Home derived from the fact that after the Common Law Procedure Acts, notices of trial not served the first day of the after-sittings in Dublin would have to remain over until the next term. The expression " after-sittings " requires some explanation, even for the modern legal reader. The greater part of the old legal year fell in the legal vacations, although the judges might be sitting on assizes, or hearing cases in Dublin at *nisi prius*. Moreover, each of the common law courts sat " in banc," and no individual judge had any general power to act for the court. As a result, a decision at *nisi prius* only became a judgment of the court on motion to the court on the first day of the term next following the verdict at *nisi prius*. These " after-sittings " were held in Dublin after the assize returned, in order to give the parties an opportunity of having judgment entered on the first day of the succeeding term. Because of the result of a delay in serving a notice of trial, a venue for the Dublin after-sittings was usually laid in some town near Dublin, Naas being frequently selected. Judge Adye Curran, who joined the Home in 1862 recalled that as many as fifty " records " would be tried at Naas at one assize.

This prosperity of the Home Circuit provoked the jealousy of its nearest neighbour, the Leinster, and a plan was evolved which did much to reduce it. At that time, Wicklow was the first town on the Leinster Circuit and, although near Dublin, was too early to catch these stray venues. The Leinster made Wicklow the last and not the first town on the circuit, and the damage was done. The railway ran right into the town of Wicklow, while the two-mile journey from Sallins station to Naas operated as a deterrent to the litigant.

The Home Circuit possessed its own form of locomotion, in the shape of a waggonette which transported its members from town to town and, like many other Irish circuits, it had its own poet laureate, Stephen Nolan Elrington, who gladdened the members by song and re-

citation. Elrington, who later became editor of *Saunders'
Newsletter*, was an accomplished versifier. When Palles
was appointed Chief Baron, in 1874, he went to one of his
first assizes on his old circuit, with Chief Justice Whiteside.
The Bar dined the judges at Naas, and Elrington's song
on the occasion contained the couplet : —

As in Avonmore and Avonbeg harmonious tides we see
A Whiteside and a Palles making a charming *vis-à-vis*.

After the dissolution of the circuit in 1885, a presentation and address, signed by all the living members, including Palles, was made to Elrington, expressing their thanks
to him for the pleasure he had given them.

Meetings of the circuit were held at Tullamore down
to 1864, and afterwards at Naas, and Palles seems to have
played a prominent part in the proceedings. Thus at the
summer meeting in Naas in 1864, a motion by Palles and
Adye Curran that members should wear their wigs and
gowns in court on circuit was defeated by seven votes to
six. Palles brought the matter up again at the spring meeting of 1869, but after some discussion it was dropped.

The business of the Home was of the type usually associated with the province of Leinster in the mid-nineteenth
century. Agrarian crime was confined to a large extent to
the county Westmeath, and the only other centre of crime
was Naas, where the proximity of the Curragh camp
tended to produce a crop of offences of varying gravity.
Civil actions included the normal litigation arising out of
the ownership of Irish land, disputed deeds and wills, and
the characteristic collection of libels and slanders. It was in
this atmosphere that the young Palles won his spurs at the
Bar. In Ireland, where specialisation has been all but unknown, a good " all-rounder " is soon at a premium. Palles
soon acquired the facile gift of case-presentation, of cross-
examination, and of accurate pleading. In the last skill, he
was a consummate master, and the few years he spent on
the Exchequer Bench before the Judicature Acts swept the

old system away showed that he could put his knowledge to good account.

It was in this way that Palles rose steadily in the practice of his profession. He soon came to be regarded by his brethren and by his professional clients as a brilliant and sound practitioner, and one of the outstanding juniors at the Bar.

VI

MARRIAGE AND SILK

As his first decade at the Bar drew to a close, Palles found himself in the fortunate position of having built up a very substantial practice on the Home Circuit. In addition, he was now attracting the attention of the Dublin solicitors to the extent of his receiving briefs in many of the more important cases at the Four Courts. His careful handling of the work and his penetrating knowledge of principle, together with his eloquent mode of address, placed his services in considerable demand and he soon found himself well established in his profession.

So long as Palles remained a stuff gownsman he does not appear to have devoted himself to any particular class of work, and the contemporary newspaper reports of proceedings at law and in equity contain references to his having been engaged in both departments. Only when he took silk did he turn his attention to the Court of Chancery to the exclusions of the other tribunals, and there he made the business of the Court his own.

It was about this time, too, that he made the acquaintance of the lady who was to become his wife. Miss Ellen Doyle and her widowed mother lived with her grand-uncle, Charles Kennedy, at Number 17, Mountjoy Square, close to the Palles household. The Kennedys were landed proprietors at Kellystown, in the county Dublin and, in addition, they possessed substantial business interests in the city. A son, Charles, had been at Clongowes with Christopher Palles, and this connection, combined with their being neighbours, made it natural that a friendship should spring up between Miss Doyle and the successful young barrister. As to the circumstances and duration of the courtship we know little; suffice it to say that they were married at the Pro-Cathedral, Marlborough Street, on 5th

August, 1862. Palles was then a little over thirty, and his bride was twenty-three.

The honeymoon was spent in Paris, and although there seems to be no substance in the legend at the Irish Bar that the bridegroom brought a copy of *Fearne on Contingent Remainders* with him to while away his leisure hours, they did find time to have their portraits painted when staying in the French capital.

At the end of the Long Vacation of 1862 they moved into Number 59, Mountjoy Square, a large house near the top of Gardiner Street, and they soon settled down to the life of a mid-Victorian Dublin family in comfortable circumstances. At this time, the Square had not yet ceased to be fashionable, and many of the houses were occupied by members of the Bar.

If the truth be told, it cannot be said that Palles's married life was an entirely unclouded one. His wife was of a naturally delicate disposition and her frequent illnesses must have been a constant source of worry to him. The real tragedy of their life together, however, was the afflicting malady of their only child, Christopher, who was born in 1863 and who lived into his ninetieth year. Of his private sorrows and disappointments Palles never spoke, and it can only be surmised that it was this aspect of his life more than any other that impelled him to dedicate himself entirely to his profession. His wife's death in 1885 brought him increased loneliness. Then, as always, he appreciated the company of young people about him. His niece Bessie, daughter of his brother Andrew, came to live with him in the big empty house, and she remained with him to the end of his long life. Bessie was an ideal companion for " The Uncle," as she always called him; ever solicitous for his welfare, managing his home with a quiet efficiency and, when fame came to him, providing for the endless round of entertainments which judges were constrained to hold in those more dignified days in Ireland. Later, she was joined in the household by his brother-in-law, Charles Kennedy, and his son Frank, the latter ultimately becoming the Chief Baron's " Associate " and confidential aide.

By 1865 Palles felt that the time had arrived when he must take that step in the career of every established junior which may end in the glory of success or in the extinction of mediocrity, and he determined to apply to the Lord Chancellor for a silk gown. Lord Palmerston's administration had now been in office since 1859, and down to 1865 he had raised to the Irish Bench four notable men, Henry George Hughes, John David FitzGerald, Rickard Deasy and Thomas O'Hagan. All had been Law Officers and all were Catholics. O'Hagan and FitzGerald both lived to receive the dignity of a peerage, the former becoming the first Catholic Lord Chancellor of Ireland since Sir Alexander Fitton in 1686, and the latter being elevated to the ultimate tribunal as a Lord of Appeal. Palmerston had restored the great seal to Maziere Brady (who had called Palles to the Bar), and it was by Brady that he was called within the Bar on 8th February, 1865.

Of the five admitted to the rank of Queen's Counsel on that day, four were to have a distinguished career in later life. Townshend ended his life as a judge of the Court of Admiralty. May became Chief Justice of the Queen's Bench and, after 1877, Lord Chief Justice of Ireland. John O'Hagan, son-in-law of his namesake, the Lord Chancellor, became the first judge of the Court of the Irish Land Commission in 1881, and is best remembered by Irish lawyers for the testamentary device that bears his name. All of them were on an average seven to ten years senior to Palles at the Bar. He was then just thirty-three years of age. Until 1865, only three men in Ireland had surpassed this feat— the precocious Isaac Butt, who took silk at thirty-one, after six years at the Bar, John David FitzGerald, who had been the same age as Butt, and the notorious William Keogh, who was a year older. It was not until 1914, when William Evelyn Wylie took silk, that the achievement was equalled.

Palmerston died in the autumn of 1865 and the short tenure of his successor, Lord John Russell, made no change in the Irish judicial establishment. The return of the Conservatives to power in 1866 under Lord Derby resulted in the retirement of Lefroy in favour of White-side, who went to the chief place in the Queen's Bench. Ireland's only Vice-Chancellor, Hedges Eyre Chatterton, was appointed in 1867 to an office for which the recipient was responsible, for Chatterton himself had initiated the necessary legislation when Attorney-General.

Before the fall of the Liberals, however, Palles had received advancement which stood him in good stead at a later date, for he was appointed one of the senior Crown prosecutors for the King's County. At this period, there were two permanent Crown counsel for each Irish county, in addition to a number of supernumeraries. Palles' senior colleague was Battersby, Q.C., while the supernumerary juniors were Longworth Dames, Adye Curran, and William O'Connor Morris. Curran later distinguished himself in being largely responsible for the detection and apprehension of the "Invincible" murderers of Lord Frederick Cavendish and Thomas Burke—the "Phoenix Park Murders"—and he ended his career as a County Court judge in the midlands. Morris, an historian of some repute, also attained the County Court bench.

It must be explained that, in Ireland, the practice of private prosecutions has never found any favour. As early as 1801, Crown solicitors responsible for prosecutions at assizes were appointed for each circuit. About 1846 the circuits began to be divided between them and by 1880 there were twenty Crown solicitors in the country. In addition, the Attorney-General about 1830 began to direct a solicitor in each county, who became termed the "Sessional Crown Solicitor," to conduct Government prosecutions at Quarter Sessions. This latter officer sometimes prosecuted at Petty Sessions also, but usually these cases were managed by the constabulary. At the end of the century it was decided to amalgamate the two offices, the first consolidation taking place in county Longford in 1902, and the process was complete by 1914. In the hands of the Crown solicitors lay the dispensing of Crown briefs, preference being given to the Crown prosecutors, so this position carried with it pecuniary advantage as well as prestige.

With his accession to the inner Bar, Palles devoted more and more of his time to the Chancery side. During the years from 1866 to 1871 there were few suits reported in that Court in which he was not engaged. With him one frequently finds associated the name of Edward Sullivan, one of the Serjeants-at-Law, whose masterly cross-examination of Major Yelverton in that *cause célèbre, Thelwall v. Yelverton,* is still cited with admiration whenever forensic skill comes up for discussion.

While it is impossible to estimate the earnings of a silk at the Irish Bar in the middle of last century, some indication of the position in the late 1860s may be gleaned from the observations of R. P. Carton, Q.C., later a County Court judge for county Clare. Writing in 1895, he said,

> "When I was called in 1863 and for nearly fifteen years afterwards the incomes of seniors of the first rank ranged from £4,000 to £6,000 per annum, and juniors from £2,000 to £3,000."

Even making allowance for the fact that Carton was attempting to paint a rosy picture of the prospects in the profession, this does afford evidence that Palles, as one of the foremost Chancery practitioners, was rapidly becoming a very rich man.

The advent of Gladstone to power in 1868 could not fail to enhance Palles's chances of further promotion. Like many Irish Catholics of the period, he belonged to that section of the Liberal party which was usually described by its opponents as " the Whigs," a section whose dominant feature was that it evinced a wholehearted belief in Irish co-operation with the English Liberals, rather than the formation of a distinct Irish party. The Whigs were particularly influential amongst the landed families and the members of the legal profession, and though their association with the architects of the Ecclesiastical Titles Bill of the early '50s had lost them some support, they had largely recovered their position in the country ten years later.

The failure of the Fenian revolt in 1867, indeed, had been due in large measure to the official Catholic view. Inspired by the sentiments of Cardinal Cullen, and those expressed by the Bishop of Kerry, that " eternity is not long enough nor hell hot enough to punish such miscreants," the great mass of the Irish people had condemned the conspiracy or had been indifferent to its implications. In England, the activities of the Fenians had made a deep impression on the public mind, and with the revulsion of feeling towards the Irish in England which characterised the Manchester executions, there was allied a feeling that, somehow, these happenings were indicative of some real defects in the policy towards Ireland. The removal of these defects was to occupy Gladstone over the next four years, and in this work Palles was to play a not inconsiderable part.

VII

LAW OFFICER OF THE CROWN

THE Parliament of 1868-1874 was the last of those of the old United Kingdom of Great Britain and Ireland until 1918 in which no distinctively organised Irish Home Rule party existed. Since the days of the Emancipation Act, the Irish members at Westminster had, on the whole, been regarded as Liberals and had supported Liberal administrations, although it was admitted by orthodox English Liberals that they, or some of them, held peculiar views which had to be taken into account. Until the extension of the franchise in 1867 the class of voters in the Irish boroughs was still more limited than in England by reason of the lower values of town properties. The more substantial Catholic farmers in rural areas who had the vote (unreduced until 1884), generally returned members of the local gentry to serve in Parliament. The Catholic clergy, too, tended to support Liberalism, not because they sympathised with its aims, but merely because it was likely to be the party which would implement their claims in the matter of educational reform. The extension of the urban franchise in 1867 gave rise to a new democratic movement in Ireland. In 1870 the Home Government Association was formed under Isaac Butt. In 1872 the passing of the Ballot Act ensured the protection of the Irish voter from overt intimidation. All these matters had their effect on the Irish political scene.

The political atmosphere existing in Ireland at the end of 1868 was an extremely complex one. The three main grievances of the majority—the position of the Established Church, land reform, and the higher education of Catholics —were under energetic review, and on disestablishment, at least, there was virtual unanimity of view. Most of the constitutionally patriotic organisations in the country were directed against the Irish Church, which was held out by them as a grave moral injustice on the great bulk of the people. The " Young Ireland " movement had never completely died; it gained strength with the defeat of Fenianism in 1867, and in common with the Irish members in Parliament, it denounced the establishment of the Church in vehement terms. Allied with it was the " National Association of Ireland," a group with pronounced ultramontane tendencies founded by Cardinal Cullen in 1864, which aimed at the twin reforms of dismembering the Church of Ireland and re-opening the university question; and through the instrumentality of John Bright, this body allied itself with the nonconformist " Liberation Society " in England, which sought the disestablishment of all the churches.

The sentiments of influential Irish Catholics received a new impetus from the events in Italy at the end of the decade. Palles appears to have shared their views at that time, for he was present at a meeting of Dublin Catholics, held on 30th November, 1870, under the chairmanship of Cardinal Cullen, " to protest against the unjustifiable invasion of the States of the Church by the Florentine Government." His identification with this wing of Catholic opinion had, as we shall see, unfortunate repercussions on his later political career.

While still in opposition, Gladstone perceived the course of coming events in Ireland and in the spring of 1868 he pronounced against the Irish Church. The general election of that year placed him in a position, with a great majority, to put that policy into effect. This he did in the session of 1869, when disestablishment was enacted into law. The next year saw the passing of the measure of agrarian reform which bore his name, a measure which, despite the faults in its application, represented an honest effort to solve once and for all the most pressing of Irish problems.

Meanwhile, events in Ireland revealed that a new spirit was abroad. The by-election of 1869-70 in county Longford, at which a Home Rule candidate, John Martin, unsuccessfully contested the seat with a clerically supported Liberal, was the beginning of the movement which resulted in the formation of the Home Government Association on 19th May, 1870. Four more elections in 1871 saw the return of Home Rule candidates in Meath, Westmeath, Galway and Limerick. The bulk of Irish Catholic opinion regarded these developments with disapproval. In its view this new departure jeopardised the achievement of Gladstone's third reform, the provision of a university acceptable to Catholics, and it did what it could to defeat what it thought was a political aberration.

During all this time the professional fortunes of the Crown prosecutor for the King's County had been prospering. His work brought him more and more to the notice of the influential elements amongst the Whigs, as a man marked out for greater things. Moreover, his appearance in the Londonderry election petition in 1868 had done much to enhance his reputation.

In 1868 the borough of Londonderry was held for the Conservatives by Lord Claud John Hamilton, son of the Marquis of Abercorn. His opponent at the election of that year was Richard Dowse, Q.C., leader of the North-West Circuit. The prospect of disestablishment secured in support of both the Presbyterians and the Catholics in Londonderry, and Dowse won the seat. Hamilton lodged a petition against his return, and the cause was heard by the election judges. The successful candidate instructed Palles to represent him at the hearing. Sir John Ross, destined to be the last Lord Chancellor of Ireland, was then a schoolboy, and he describes the scene in Londonderry court-house in his memoirs:

> " Things had been going badly for the elected member; the counsel for the petitioner looked gay and triumphant. Serious evidence had been given tending to prove what, in law, amounted to bribery by one of Mr. Dowse's agents. The respondent himself appeared to be unnerved and almost on the point of breaking down. Then his leading counsel, Mr. Palles, Q.C., rose and commenced his argument on the effect of the evidence. Neither before nor since have I heard anything like it. The clear, precise sentences rang out, dominating the situation. Every interruption on

the part of the enemy was met by a lightning thrust, that laid the interrupter prostrate.

" The tide of battle had been suddenly turned by this wonderful advocate. The petitioner's counsel relapsed from triumph into depression; the other counsel for the respondent became jubilant in their turn. The effect on me was electric. I was seized with a passion to become a great advocate like Mr. Palles."

Ross, whose future career was influenced in this dramatic way, did achieve fame on the Irish Bench, and formed a lifelong friendship with Palles. Their close connection was emphasised by the fact that they both received honorary degrees from their old University in 1914.

It was at the by-election in county Meath in January, 1871 that Palles made his first entry into active political life. The sitting Liberal member, Mathew Corbally, had died towards the end of the previous year and it became necessary to select his successor. Corbally was a Whig who for many years had shared the representation of Meath with Frederick Lucas (founder of the *Tablet*). Cardinal Cullen entirely approved of Corbally's politics, and the local clergy favoured the return of his nephew, the Hon. George Plunkett, a landed proprietor in the county and a brother of Lord Fingall. Plunkett was willing to stand, and in his election address, issued on 5th December, 1870, he proclaimed himself a supporter of the " principles of Liberalism," an advocate of denominational education for Catholics, and a firm opponent of the attacks on the Papal States.

There were, however, other influences at work. On the day Plunkett's address appeared, there also appeared in the Dublin newspapers another address, directed to " The independent electors and people of Meath." It was issued from Number 59, Mountjoy Square and was signed by Christopher Palles. In its contents, it bore a marked similarity to that of the other candidate, its author declaring that

" I regard the usurpation by Victor Emmanual of the territory of the Pope as a violation of law human and divine . . . No effort of mine, either in or out of Parliament, shall be wanting to restore it."

He went on to urge the " application of the denominational system to primary, intermediate and university education," holding that " religious equality cannot exist in Ireland unless Catholics shall fully participate in all institutions."

The advent of the second candidate placed the electors of Meath in a position of great difficulty. While it could be argued that the Whigs in general, and Cardinal Cullen in particular, may have felt that a prominent Catholic barrister stood a better chance of success than a local man chosen on the dynastic principle, it is more likely that Palles's intervention was caused by his own personal choice, stimulated, perhaps, by his friends' advice. In those days party organisation was still a loose-knit affair, and the appearance of stray " independent " candidates was not unknown at elections.

These difficulties were stressed by the parish priest of Duleek, Father Gaughrin, in a letter to the *Irish Times* on 7th December. After commenting on the fact that the addresses of the two aspirants were " curiously coincident," the writer observed that " both belong to a profession which in the political world is justly suspected," and he suggested that lawyers should stop using parliamentary seats in Ireland as stepping-stones to preferment. Next day the same newspaper expressed editorial approval of the sentiments aired by the worthy parish priest, stating that the practice resulted in the " corruption of political life in this country and the growing demoralisation of an important and honourable profession." It went on:

" Mr. Palles has attained, by sheer dint of merit, a very high place in his profession."

The promotion which he sought, it was said,

" is a promotion which is his by right, and which would be accorded to him as a matter of course if judicial preferments were, as they ought to be, the prizes of professional superiority. But it is not professional merit that will get Mr. Palles into Parliament nor is it merit of any kind, but mere subserviency to one Government or another which will help him from Parliament to the Bench."

Such strictures—which might well be applied to conditions in Ireland ninety years later—had a decisive effect on the second candidate. On 9th December, Palles issued a further statement to the Meath electors, in which he announced his retirement from the contest, in order to prevent a split in the Liberal ranks. The *Irish Times,* after reiterating its objection to " handing over Irish constituencies to lawyers," indicated its feelings for the person concerned by saying that it

" would be glad that some constituency regarding Mr. Palles as an able and distinguished Irishman should select him as their representative . . ."

This was an inauspicious beginning to a political career and, in the event, the seat was won by the Home Rule candidate, John Martin, an Ulster Presbyterian who had been transported after the 1848 rising, and who had already put up a sturdy fight against the Whigs in county Longford. His success by almost two to one was probably due to the fact that the Meath clergy were divided in their loyalties, or, at least, because they did not attempt to sway the voters in favour of Plunkett. Martin held the seat until his death, when he was succeeded by Charles Stewart Parnell.

The Meath affair had one important effect on Palles's later fortunes. His prompt withdrawal in order to present an unbroken front to Home Rule indicated to the Government that he was at least entitled to consideration when the time came for promotions and advancements.

The retention of the Londonderry seat by Dowse after the unsuccessful petition of 1868 resulted in his being appointed Solicitor-General for Ireland in January, 1870. The Attorney-General was Charles Robert Barry, Q.C. Two years later, in January, 1872, Barry was raised to the

Court of Queen's Bench, and Dowse succeeded him as the senior Law Officer. This created a vacancy in the office of Solicitor-General, and it seemed that the logical successor was Hugh Law, Q.C., who had been Law Adviser to the Government—an office created earlier in the century —since 1868. Law was senior to Palles by over ten years at the Bar, though he had not taken silk until 1860; and his services to the Liberal cause in Ireland were beyond reproach.

The Chief Secretary for Ireland, the Marquis of Hartington, did not appoint Law. He sent for Christopher Palles. On 7th February, 1872, Palles was sworn in as Her Majesty's Solicitor-General for Ireland. The offer had been made to him and had been accepted on 29th January, and the necessary letters patent had been issued on that day. On 8th February, the new Solicitor-General was called upon to take his place in the Court of Appeal in Chancery by the Lord Chancellor, Lord O'Hagan. Two days later, he was leading counsel in the last episode of the notorious proceedings against Robert Kelly in connection with the shooting of Head-Constable Talbot. At an earlier trial, Kelly had been arraigned for the murder of Talbot, and had been defended by Isaac Butt. Butt had convinced the jury that Talbot's death had been caused not by gunshot wounds, but by the subsequent treatment which he had received from a well-known Dublin surgeon, and had secured an acquittal. Now, assisted by the exertions of Serjeant Armstrong and the "Green Street team" of Crown prosecutors, William O'Brien and James Murphy, Palles obtained a conviction on the lesser charge of attempted murder.

The new appointment was an extremely popular one, and the *Irish Law Times* of 28th February, 1872, reflected contemporary opinion of the new Law Officer's merits when it said that

> " no one could have been more completely fit for the high position, in every sense of legal knowledge, high moral tone and uprightness and professional eminence . . . his unflinching perseverance in asserting the rights of his

client being only equalled by his courtesy to his brethren and his respect for the Court."

When we come to examine the reasons impelling Hartington to make the appointment, a number of difficulties emerge. Palles had made for himself an outstanding reputation at the Bar, it is true, but he was still a young man, being then just in his fortieth year. His contributions to the party had been of a high order, but then, so had been those of Hugh Law. A number of solutions present themselves. First, the Liberals probably desired that at least one of the Law Officers should be a Catholic, and when Barry was raised to the Bench, Palles may have been brought in to restore the balance. Palles, moreover, enjoyed the close friendship of Cardinal Cullen, whose powerful influence it was thought prudent to appease. Secondly, Hartington had had a very recent opportunity of assessing the merits of his new Solicitor-General, in the affair of the Phoenix Park riots.

In August, 1871, it had been announced that a meeting would be held at the Wellington Monument in Phoenix Park, outside Dublin, to agitate for the release of certain "political prisoners still confined in English dungeons." An application was made to the secretary of the Board of Works (which controlled the Park), for permission to erect a platform, and this was refused. It happened that the Prince of Wales and other members of the Royal Family were staying with the Lord-Lieutenant, Earl Spencer, at the Vice-Regal Lodge in the Park, and the leading popular newspaper had stated that it was

> "intolerable that alien princes should come here in search of a welcome while the power they represent still holds fifty patriots in prison."

The meeting was attempted, and there was a serious collision with the police. Certain spectators were injured, and actions for assault were commenced against Hartington, T. H. Burke, the Under-Secretary, and others.

The actions came on for hearing in February, 1872, in

the Court of Exchequer, before Chief Baron Pigot and a special jury. Isaac Butt, Q.C., led for the plaintiffs, while Dowse and Palles represented Hartington.

One of the allegations made by the defence was that the Park was not a " public place," and so the Government had been justified in prohibiting the meeting there. Palles, who took little part in the cross-examination of witnesses, directed a powerful legal argument towards establishing this proposition, and he soon found himself crossing swords with the redoubtable Butt.

In opening the defence Palles was able to display his powers of advocacy to the full, and even now, reading the dry pages of the report nearly ninety years later, the speech is a most convincing one. After reviewing the evidence, he went on to conclude:

> " As far as Lord Hartington is concerned, the case is practically at an end. You may hear some ingenious observations from Mr. Butt. He is always able—he is always ingenious—and sometimes, gentlemen, I think he is so able that he succeeds in convincing his own better judgment, and in overcoming his own sound apprehension of legal and constitutional law.

The plea was in vain, and the jury returned a verdict against Hartington in the sum of £25. On further argument, Chief Baron Pigot reserved leave to have the verdict set aside in order to avoid a new trial, since the first had lasted five months. After much delay the case came on before Barons Deasy and FitzGerald in 1876, who reversed the finding and entered judgment for the Marquis. On appeal to the Exchequer Chamber, this was affirmed in May, 1877, over five years after the occurrence.

Hartington, however, had ample reason to be grateful to Palles, who had defended him so ably, and it can scarcely be doubted that when the opportunity of promoting his advocate presented itself just before the case came on for hearing, he availed himself of it. In addition, he was later to show his gratitude in a more important matter.

Unlike the practice in England, it was customary for the Attorney-General to be a member of the Irish Privy

Council, but not the Solicitor-General. The latter seems to have been summoned to the Council from time to time for consultation, however, for Palles is recorded as having attended a meeting on 8th March, 1872. In Ireland, indeed, the influence of the Law Officers was always exercised in a more direct manner than in England. Since the Attorney-General was invariably a Privy Councillor, he was frequently consulted by the Lord-Lieutenant on the general policy of administration. An example of this is to be seen in the case of Blackburne in 1841. He advised that Brewster be made Law Advisor to the Irish Government. This produced a storm of protest from O'Connell and his party, but Blackburne remained firm and, as his biographer put it, "intimated to the Lord Chancellor that he would not tolerate the refusal to ratify his selection." In Melbourne's time, the Irish Attorney-General was described as being "a great mixture of law and of general political reasoning."

About the time of Palles's appointment, one finds a curious incident, which was probably unique in Irish legal annals. The usual practice then was to elect the Law Officers as Benchers of King's Inns, if they did not already hold that office. Accordingly, Palles was duly elected to the Bench on 15th April, 1872. Next day, he wrote to the Benchers, thanking them for the honour which they had conferred on him, but declining it because of "the question at issue" between the Inns and the Bar of Ireland, while he was still a member of the Council of the latter body.

The story underlying this incident is an extremely interesting one, and is that of a quarrel between the Benchers and the Bar of some three years' standing. For a number of years, it seems, considerable dissatisfaction had been felt by the members of the practising Bar because of the attitude of the Benchers in electing to their number persons who could not in any sense be described as representatives of the profession. At a general meeting of the Bar, held at the Four Courts on 5th June, 1869, indeed, Palles himself had proposed a resolution to the effect that the "Govern ing Body of the Irish Bar ought to be remodelled so as to effectively represent the profession," and a committee of which he was a member was appointed to open negotiations with the Benchers of King's Inns. A long correspondence followed, from which it appears that the situation had developed in which barristers were in the minority on the Bench, due mainly to the fact that there were many ex-members of the judiciary who continued to retain their places as Benchers after they had retired from office.

A suggestion from the Bar that this state of affairs violated the rules of King's Inns as laid down in 1793 was met by a downright refusal on the part of the Benchers either to allow the Bar committee to inspect their records or even to meet them in conference, and relations between the two bodies underwent a rapid and progressive deterioration. A further suggestion that the outer Bar might be given places on the Bench of the Inns was summarily rejected, and the Bar committee then proceeded to recommend that an application be made to the legislature for a statute to establish the constitution of King's Inns on such a basis as would restore to the profession in Ireland the right of self government " and protect this right from future encroachments."

In pursuance of this, the papers were duly sent to the Chief Secretary, with the suggestion that the the whole affair might be referred to the Royal Commission then being established to investigate the relations existing between King's Inns and the solicitors' profession in Ireland. This was in April, 1870, but the matter dragged on for another two years, and was no nearer resolution when Palles was appointed Solicitor-General. In the end, the Benchers voluntarily reformed their constitution, and Palles's deferred election as a Bencher took place on 2nd November, 1872.

Official duties soon occupied all his time and attention. At the beginning of January, the elevation of Viscount Castlerosse to the peerage as Lord Kenmare created a parliamentary vacancy in county Kerry. Mr. Dease stood as a Government candidate, with the full support of the moderate Catholics. He was opposed by Mr. Blenner-hassett, whose claim to the seat was pressed by the Home Rulers. Lord Kenmare wrote to Hartington that " it is essential that troops should be in the county a week before the election. The intimidation is tremendous, and their presence would give confidence." The Catholic Bishop of Kerry pressed for similar assistance, " especially cavalry." Troops were sent, and a gunboat was dispatched to Valentia to protect the tenants of the Knight of Kerry. These precautions were in vain, and Dease was defeated by a large majority. Polling day was marked by scenes of the wildest enthusiasm. At Tralee, the ballot was signalised by " the carrying in of a patriarchal voter named Kissane, whose age was set down at the fabulous figure of 114." The election was immediately impeached by a petition being lodged.

At the same time, the representation of Galway county was being contested and, there, other issues besides Home Rule seem to have intruded on the electoral fray. The struggle was one between the landed gentry and the Catholic clergy. All the latter, from the Archbishop of Tuam down to the youngest curate, were arrayed on the side of the Home Ruler, Captain Nolan, while Liberal and Conservative landlords of every denomination united to support Captain Trench. Again, the Home Ruler triumphed, and the customary petition was lodged.

The petition against Captain Nolan's return was heard at Galway by Mr. Justice Keogh. Keogh had already made himself infamous in the eyes of the popular party in Ireland by his dramatic defection from the " Pope's Brass Band," or Independent Irish Party, in 1852, in order to accept office in the administration of Lord Aberdeen. The fact that before this betrayal he had received the support of Cullen and the clergy did nothing to minimise his crime in popular eyes.

Already, in 1869, Palles had come into collision with Keogh, in the proceedings arising out of the Youghal election petition of that year. It had been sought to attach a solicitor named Barry because the *Cork Examiner* had published a speech of his, criticising Keogh's decision on the petition. Keogh, on his own initiative, had cited Barry to appear before the Common Pleas, and the latter had been defended by Butt, Thomas O'Hagan, and Palles. It was on that occasion that Butt made the speech which has become a classic, castigating the conduct of Keogh, and ending with the words: " Be Kent unmannerly when Lear is mad."

Keogh gave his decision on the Galway petition in a judgment which occupied nine consecutive hours in its delivery. He unseated Nolan on the grounds that his election had been procured by undue influence and clerical intimidation.

The judgment was delivered in an extremely biassed manner, and did little to enhance the reputation of the judiciary. Forty-five pages of it were devoted to an analysis of the conduct of a number of individual priests in the election, and as witnesses before him. He stated that the Archbishop of Tuam, the Bishop of Galway, the Bishop of Clonfert, and all the clergy had been guilty of " an organised attempt to defeat the free franchise and the free votes " of the electors. He added that the election presented " the most astonishing attempt at ecclesiastical tyranny which the whole history of priestly intolerance afforded," and he spoke of Nolan's great crowd of supporters as " mindless cowards, instruments in the hands of ecclesiastical despots."

The fact that Keogh continued to exhibit on the Bench increasing symptoms of eccentricity (he died in Germany, by his own hand, after attempting the life of his valet), explains but does not excuse his conduct at Galway, and there can seldom have been any popular outburst of excitement and hatred in Ireland to equal that which was directed at him after the decision. The Catholic clergy, under the presidency of Cardinal Cullen, published a long protest in the form of an address to the Catholics of Dublin, and Keogh's subsequent progress through the country on circuit necessitated the most stringent precautions being taken for his personal safety.

Meanwhile, the Government found itself in considerable difficulty. It was seeking to placate the Catholics, yet it could hardly ignore the charges levelled against their clergy by Keogh, notwithstanding the intemperate manner of their presentation. The fact that in June the Court of Common Pleas, by a majority of three to one, upheld the judgment unseating Nolan, merely strengthened the official view that action would have to be taken, and in this the House of Commons endorsed the Government's attitude by defeating heavily a motion for Keogh's removal. The Law Officers, Dowse and Palles, were now directed to prepare indictments against twenty of the Galway clergy, including the Bishop of Clonfert, Dr. Duggan.

Palles found himself confronted with a most serious moral question. As a devout Catholic, he was aware of a general provision of canon law, which had been re-stated as recently as 1869, creating penalties for Catholics who obliged lay judges to bring ecclesiastics before secular tribunals. His own expert knowledge of the common law could not help him here, and he took the opinion of a Jesuit friend who was a skilled canonist. He was advised that although this was a general ecclesiastical law, the existence of a recognised canonical custom in Ireland to the contrary precluded its application to the laity. Moreover, he was assured, even if the pontifical constitution had applied in Ireland, it would not extend to such a case as his; and he might proceed to indict the bishop and the priests without fear of ecclesiastical censure.

This opinion satisfied Palles, so far as it went, but a further problem remained to trouble him. Even though such an action on his part might be lawful, was it expedient? Would it have an adverse effect on the Church of which he was a loyal member? There was but one course open to him. He sought the opinion of Cardinal Cullen, and he did so in a written submission, accompanied by his resignation from the office of Solicitor-General. The submission contained a request to the

Cardinal to forward the latter to the Chief Secretary if after reflection, he considered that the circumstances warranted it. It need only be said here that Cullen returned the instrument of resignation to Palles, and it was never dispatched to its destination.

It was not until February, 1873, that the cases came on for hearing, before Chief Justice Whiteside and a jury. By then, Palles had succeeded Dowse as Attorney-General, and he led John Ball, Q.C., for the prosecution.

The first prisoner arraigned was Father Loftus, and the excitement was so intense that the public had to be excluded from Court. After a hearing of two days, at which evidence was given to show that Father Loftus had incited a mob against a magistrate, the Chief Justice charged the jury for a period of three hours. They then retired, and being unable to agree on a verdict after three hours, they were discharged. The Bishop of Clonfert was then put up, and he was acquitted by the Dublin jury after six minutes deliberation. Scenes of the wildest enthusiasm outside the Court followed the announcement of this verdict, and in reply to Whiteside, Palles stated that the Crown had decided not to proceed with any of the other cases " at present." In fact, nothing further was heard of the Galway prosecutions, and what must have been an extremely painful episode for Palles came to an end.

The summer of 1872 brought the death of Baron Hughes of the Exchequer. Dowse was elevated to replace him at the beginning of the following term, and in accordance with the normal practice Palles was promoted Attorney-General. On the afternoon of 4th November, 1872, he presented himself before the Lord Chancellor in chambers and was duly sworn in by the Clerk of the Hanaper. In his place, the Government appointed Hugh Law, Q.C.

A most awkward political crisis now developed. Dowse had held the borough of Londonderry since 1868, having been re-elected in 1870 on his appointment as Solicitor-General. Whilst he had held office much of his time was spent in London, attending to the parliamentary business of the Irish Government and, by tradition as well as by virtual necessity, one if not both of the Irish Law Officers must hold seats in the Commons. Now, neither Palles nor Law were members of Parliament, and there was no one in the House competent to answer for Irish legal affairs.

The Liberals had already selected a candidate for the Londonderry seat left vacant by Dowse, in the person of Dr. Evory Kennedy, an eminent Dublin obstetrician. He was now asked to withdraw in favour of Palles, who was plunged into his first parliamentary campaign. In the event, it proved to be his last.

VIII

THE BOROUGH OF LONDONDERRY

The opening of the campaign for the representation of the Maiden City was not long delayed. On the very day on which Palles was sworn Attorney-General, *The Times* was able to report that he was to offer himself as a successor to Dowse, "with a fair chance of success," though as that newspaper was careful to point out

> "he will have difficulties with the Presbyterian electors . . . They control Derry and are hostile to the denominational system of education of which Palles has spoken strongly in favour in addressing another constituency."

This was, doubtless, a reference to the abortive address to the Meath electors, in which he had put forward the claims of Catholics to university education.

The political situation in Londonderry was somewhat complex. There were three main parties. First, there were the members of the Church of Ireland, who were Conservative to a man. Secondly, there was a large Presbyterian section of the electorate, the majority of whom supported the principles of Gladstonian Liberalism. Lastly, there was the Catholic voter, who was a Liberal, with the exception of a small and insignificant proportion of Home Rulers. The combination of Presbyterian and Catholic was an irresistible one. In 1868 they had enabled Dowse to wrest the seat from the hands of Hamilton, having been stimulated to do so by the prospect of disestablishment. Now that this had been carried through, and the measure of agrarian reform included in the Land Act of 1870 had been granted, the remaining Gladstonian reform, university education, was the burning topic of domestic policy with the Irish electorate. It was vital, therefore, that Palles should be able to assure the Presbyterian section of his supporters that they had nothing to fear in this quarter.

Two days after his induction as Attorney-General, Palles left Dublin for the scene of action, and on the evening of 6th November, he had a long conference with his supporters in the borough. The Conservatives were already in the field. They had selected a London solicitor, Charles E. Lewis, to represent them, but they soon ran into trouble. The local Conservative organisation, resenting the intrusion of what they regarded as a " carpet bagger," were ready to nominate their own candidate, Bartholomew McCorkell, a local landlord, for the vacancy, and it looked as if the electorate would be confronted with two rival aspirants. Lewis' primary qualification for the seat was his ostentatious Presbyterianism. He had sought to be adopted at Belfast in 1868, without success, a cynical commentator observing that "He was said to have been a Presbyterian for two years; he asserted that he had at least been one for six." In addition, the Home Rulers, encouraged by their recent successes and aware of the potentialities of attempting to drive a wedge between the Catholic voters on the issue of the Galway election prosecutions, prepared to put forward Joseph G. Biggar. The *Irish Times,* after referring with undisguised contempt to the chances of " an adventurous stranger such as Mr. Lewis, the London solicitor," observed that

> " Mr. Palles has never taken a line of politics which could in the slightest way be deemed offensive by any party. He never adopted extreme views, or countenanced a factious proceeding. . . . As against Mr. Lewis, Mr. Palles might count on unusual support."

The first shots of the campaign were fired by Lewis. At a largely attended meeting in the city on 7th November, he accused Palles of having told the electors of Meath that Victor Emmanuel was the " usurper " of the Vatican lands. He followed this up with a more telling allegation, namely that the Liberal candidate had been on the platform with Cardinal Cullen in Dublin, at the meeting which had advocated the establishment of a Catholic university. Lewis's meeting appears to have been a lively one, a number of Home Rulers being present, for we read that " a man cried for ' Home Rule ' and was badly injured."

The inaugural meeting of the Liberals, held on the previous evening, was a stormy affair. Many Home Rulers were present, and the proceedings were punctuated by cries of: " No priest hunter!," " Away with the prosecutor of the priests!," and similar offensive remarks. Dealing with his interrupters, Palles fearlessly admitted that the Galway prosecutions instituted by his predecessor, Dowse, had his complete sanction and support, and he rather astutely reminded his listeners that

> " The Archbishop of Tuam and the Bishop of Clonfert and others petitioned to be prosecuted, and Mr. Mitchell Henry complained that the prosecutions were too few."

Next day came his election address, which was published in the newspapers on 11th November. It deserves to be quoted at length, as indicating the tactics of the author:

> ". . . I am not altogether unknown in Londonderry. I have had large and cordial relations with many of its citizens and I have received the most gratifying proofs of their regard.
>
> " But I come before you now, having by the favour of my Sovereign assumed the post of first Law Officer of the Crown in Ireland under Mr. Gladstone's administration, and I ask you to return me to Parliament, not so much for any merits of my own, as because I am identified in principle and feeling with the policy of that great statesman and because you will thus declare your appreciation of his services in the past and your confidence in his purposes in the future.
>
> " I need only point to the Church Act, which has established religious equality—to the Land Act, which has given so much security to the tenancy of Ireland; and to the concession of the ballot, by which it has been assured for the first time the free and honest exercise of the elective franchise. . . .
>
> " I desire earnestly an opportunity of demonstrating my devotion to those great principles and to that sacred cause; and therefore I seek the distinguished honour of becoming your representative."

This manifesto was described by *The Times* as being
" calm and conciliatory in its tone and happily combining
clearness of expression with judicious reticence." The electors were " prudently left to conjecture what the purposes
of the Government may be in relation to certain delicate
matters."

It is hardly necessary to recall what these " delicate
matters " were: on the question of university education
Palles had preserved an enigmatic silence, and Lewis's
charges of his being identified with the views of Cardinal
Cullen remained unanswered. While one cannot go as far
as the Dublin *Daily Express,* which declared that " no man
has identified himself so much with the principles of
advanced ultramontanism as Palles," nevertheless, in the
light of his connection with the earlier Meath contest, one
feels that the electors of Londonderry were justified in
continuing to regard Palles's suitability as their representative with some reserve.

The advent of Biggar and his associates added to the
Attorney-General's troubles. From the outset the Home
Rule campaign was conducted on the footing that the
Catholic vote must be split. With this in view, Biggar said
that he was quite willing to withdraw from the contest if
Palles would withdraw the Galway prosecutions, a course
which the latter was manifestly unable to pursue. The
Catholic voters, awaiting the guidance of their clergy,
found the latter placed in a quandary. An open invitation
by the clergy to support Palles would appear like a betrayal
of their Galway brethren; any condemnation of the Liberal
candidate would result in a Conservative victory.

Biggar followed up his initial assault with a series of
most venomous written and spoken attacks. One of his
posters read:

> " Who is likely to attain the judgeship which will prob-
> ably be vacant in four months? Palles, of course, as a
> reward for defeating the cause of Ireland in Derry!"

This was probably a reference to the ageing Chief Baron
Pigot, whose retirement was then being canvassed, and

whom Palles was ultimately to succeed in the spring of 1874.

Meanwhile the local Conservative, McCorkell, remained unmoved by the blandishments of Lewis's supporters, and faced by heavy pressure, he refused to withdraw. Support for the two men was almost evenly divided, and the *Irish Times* had been near the truth when it had said that there was only lukewarm enthusiasm in Londonderry for the London solicitor.

Nomination day was Wednesday, 20th November, 1872. The four candidates duly handed in their papers. Palles' papers were signed by William Tillie, the High Sheriff, and John O'Neill, J.P., while his supporters were the Most Revd. Dr. Kelly, Catholic Bishop of Derry, David Watt, William F. Biggar, Thomas A. White, Joseph Orr, Charles O'Neill, Alexander Black, and Peter T. Rodgers. His supporters were carefully chosen, five being Catholics, four Presbyterians, and one a member of the Church of Ireland. On the previous Sunday, indeed, speculation in the city had been rife. It had been thought that the priests would " speak out " for Palles in the churches, but they had remained silent. Biggar's agitation had done its work.

All was now in train for the election, the first ever to be held in Ireland under the secret ballot. On Thursday, it was reported, " an extra force of two hundred policemen has been ordered here, but judging from the total absence of excitement, their services will hardly be required." That evening, the Home Rulers held their final rally, and were addressed by A. M. Sullivan, who had travelled from Dublin to support Biggar. He made a most savage attack on Palles, denouncing him as " the liveried servant of the Castle, who went there with religion on his lips and perfidy in his heart." " His name would go down in history," declared Sullivan, " as the greatest Judas that had ever sold his country and his God." On Friday night, he followed this up with another impassioned oration, in which he challenged the Attorney-General to declare his views on the education question.

On the same evening, Palles made his final appeal at a

meeting at the court-house. After Mr. Hampton, " formerly an ardent Apprentice Boy, now converted to Liberal views," had exhorted " his fellow-Protestants " to vote for Palles, the latter spoke at some length. He said that the issue to be decided was whether the Government of Mr. Gladstone had or had not their confidence. The struggle was between him and Mr. Lewis, " the pious attorney from London and nominee of the Duke of Abercorn." He replied to the philippic of Sullivan, stigmatised the charges brought against him as false, and challenged Sullivan to substantiate them. The meeting ended on an optimistic note, it being reported next morning that " the Roman Catholic clergy were now using their influence with their people to induce them to keep together in support of Mr. Palles . . ." The Conservatives were still divided between Lewis and McCorkell, and it looked as if Dowse's victories of 1868 and 1870 were to be repeated on the morrow.

But the result of the ballot on Saturday, 23rd November, was predetermined by the events of the previous night. At a meeting of the Conservatives a poll of McCorkell's supporters and those of Lewis resulted in a majority for the London solicitor, and the local man withdrew. A united Conservative electorate now faced Palles and his supporters, weakened as they were by the Home Rule tactics and, it is to be feared, by the reluctance of the Attorney-General himself to make an unequivocal statement of his position on the education issue. When the poll closed on Saturday evening, the result was, Lewis: 606; Palles: 552; Biggar: 89. Londonderry had been lost for the Gladstonians.

A number of factors contributed to this result. For the Home Rulers, A. M. Sullivan, we have seen, accused the Liberal candidate of having abandoned the cause of denominational education, to which, as the favourite of the Catholic Bishops, he was thought to be devoted. Sullivan's statement, published in the Catholic *Derry Journal*, to the effect that Palles had " betrayed his country and his God," was withdrawn by the author a week after the election, when he stated he believed that he did not use the last words as reported, " and his God." The Attorney-General, it seems, might be a traitor to his country but not to his God; but the harm was done.

Another attack had come from an unexpected quarter, when the Nationalist newspaper in Belfast supported by the Catholic bishop, Dr. Dorrien, condemned Palles. Dorrien was in disagreement with Dr. Cullen over Home Rule, having presided at a Home Rule meeting in the Dublin archdiocese when the latter forbade any of his clergy to take part. Nevertheless, it was a little odd to see him opposed to the candidate who had the support of the Catholic Bishop of Derry. According to the testimony of Lord O'Hagan, in the heat of the contest Cullen had written to Dorrien, expressing the hope that he had had nothing to do with the Belfast newspaper attack on Palles, and declaring that such articles were " a disgrace to Catholicism." Dorrien, it is said, disclaimed all responsibility, but it afterwards transpired that the reputed editor of the newspaper was one of Dorrien's own curates, Father Michael Cahill. When the paper changed hands at a later date, indeed, it appeared that the bishop had advanced £2,000 for its support and was thus at the time of the Londonderry election its virtual proprietor. In the circumstances, it is difficult to see how the Bishop of Down and Connor could disclaim responsibility for its attack on Palles.

Writing on the Monday following the declaration of the poll, the *Irish Times* reminded its readers that the election had been one of immense interest, not only from the fact that it was the first ever to be held in Ireland under the Ballot Act, but also because

> " one of the candidates was the first Law Officer of the Crown, who, in a professional career of unsurpassed brilliancy, had won the respect and good opinion of men of every party."

It is to be feared, however, that he was quite unable to gain the confidence of the Presbyterian electors of Londonderry. His failure to refute adequately the charges of sympathy with Dr. Cullen's educational views, his unfortunate intervention in the earlier Meath election and, above all, his religion, rendered him suspect. In addition, the part he had to play with regard to the Galway prosecutions tended to estrange him from some of the more bigoted members of his own church, and to lay him open to the attacks of the Home Rulers. These defects would have been absent in the case of Dr. Evory Kennedy, himself a native of Londonderry, or in the case of the Solicitor-General, Hugh Law.

That the Presbyterians themselves were divided is apparent from the remarks of Lewis at his victory meeting, when he condemned the conduct of " certain clergymen and certain professors " who, after denouncing denominational education, supported Palles, " the pronounced advocate of that system." This was probably a reference to Magee College, Londonderry, an institution of higher learning which had been founded by those Presbyterians who favoured denominationalism in education.

In the defeat at the hands of the electorate of Londonderry, however, there lay the seeds of a later victory. If Palles had won the seat, it can scarcely be doubted that his valuable services to the Liberals in opposition would have prevented his judicial preferment in 1874. As it happened, he ceased to be of any political use to his supporters and so he was saved for the service of the common law.

IX

LORD CHIEF BARON

THE rejection of Palles by the electors of Londonderry was a serious blow to the prestige of the Liberals in Ireland. The intervention of Biggar, the embarrassment of the Galway prosecutions, the doubts about Gladstone's plans for the new university, all had conspired to bring about his defeat. Now the Government found itself without a legal representative in the Commons for Irish affairs. Lawson, Sullivan, Barry and Dowse were already on the Bench. Hugh Law had still to obtain a seat. As a result, much of Palles's and Law's time during 1873 was spent in journeying to and from London, sitting in the House " under the clock," and advising the Government on the many Irish legal problems confronting them.

There were also legal preoccupations at home. In February Palles was undertaking the distasteful task of prosecuting the Galway bishops and clergy. In addition, he conducted the prosecution as Attorney-General in the three trials at Omagh assizes of District Inspector Montgomery, of the Royal Irish Constabulary, who had been charged with the murder of the cashier of the Northern Bank in Newtown-Stewart, William Glass.

Newtown-Stewart is a small town in the county Tyrone, about ten miles from Omagh. There is a branch of the Northern Bank in the town, and at the time of these happenings, the ground floor portion of the premises was used as a bank, the rest being the manager's private residence.

On 29th June, 1871, the manager was absent on business; his wife and family were away on holiday, and the only occupant of the bank was William Glass, the cashier, whose duty it was to close the office at 3.00 p.m. Between three and a quarter-past three, sounds resembling the pushing of a chair and a groan, were heard emanating from the bank. A short time afterwards, the manager's servant went into the hall to see the office clock, but on looking through the glazed door she saw a pool of blood. She raised the alarm and the body of Glass was found lying face downwards in the office. There were twelve wounds in the head, several of them fatal. No weapon was found. The motive was apparently robbery, for a large sum of money in notes and gold had been removed.

Police enquiries of a most vigorous kind were immediately set on foot by the officer commanding the constabulary in Newtown-Stewart, Thomas Hartley Montgomery. Montgomery was a man of great ability, with a special knowledge of banking, having in his early life been employed in a bank himself. He knew the premises well, having been a friend of the murdered Glass and also a friend of the manager, and had visited the premises on the day of the murder. He represented the Crown at the coroner's inquest which opened on the next day.

One of the witnesses called had been present, as a magistrate, at the examination of the body. He stated that it was clear that the murderer was no stranger to the premises; that he must have been aware of the absence of the manager and must have been a friend of the cashier, as there was evidence of some talking being heard in the inner office, just before the bank closed. He then created a sensation by declaring that nobody answered these conditions except one man, and that man was Inspector Montgomery himself. This suggestion was ridiculed. Montgomery immediately offered himself as a witness, but the coroner deemed it unnecessary to take his statement. It then appeared that the Inspector when leaving the bank on the day of the crime carried a waterproof coat over his arm. A member of the jury suggested that the absence of blood on the murderer's clothes could be accounted for if he had worn the coat when striking the fatal blows. This suggestion, which appears to have been without foundation, seemed to impress the jury, for they found that the murder had been committed by the District Inspector.

Montgomery was arrested, his residence was searched and the clothes worn by him on the day in question were sent for analysis. No trace of blood was found on the clothes, but further investigations revealed that he was in serious financial difficulties. A reward offered by the bank resulted in the greater part of the money and the weapon —a loaded billhook—being found in the Grange Wood, near the town. It further appeared that Montgomery had been three times at the Grange Wood within twelve hours after the crime. As a result, he was duly returned for trial at the next Spring Assizes for the county Tyrone. This trial, before Mr. Justice Lawson, resulted in a disagreement. At the Summer Assizes he was again put on trial before Mr. Justice Barry, and this jury also failed to agree. The judge went on to finish the North-West Circuit, and returned to Omagh for the third trial.

Palles prosecuted in person. His opening statement to the jury was a masterpiece of lucidity. Perhaps its most remarkable feature was its moderation: it was really an understatement and the facts, when they were brought out, were far more telling than if there had been a full statement emphasising the salient points of the case. With Palles was Richard Armstrong, Q.C., First Serjeant-at-Law, a powerful advocate.

For the prisoner, Francis Macdonagh, Q.C., led George Keys. Macdonagh was then at the pinnacle of success at the Bar and, as we have seen, he had encountered Palles early in the latter's career. He was a superb actor, and had a low, impressive and most distinct voice, being linked with Curran and Seymour Bushe as one of the greatest of Irish forensic orators. Fastidious in dress—he always wore lavender kid gloves in court—he combined a dignity of manner with a certain lack of scruple which ultimately proved to be his professional undoing. His two defences of Montgomery were, first, that it was quite impossible for him to have walked down the street of Newtown-Stewart, concealing the weapon and the money; secondly, that the murderer must have been covered in blood, and no trace of blood was found on the prisoner's clothing.

At the beginning of the second trial, Palles had called a sergeant of the R.I.C., the exact height of the accused and wearing the clothes worn by him on the day of the murder. He was asked to stand up in the witness box—in Ireland, witnesses gave evidence seated—and then Palles asked him if he had concealed about him the money and the murder weapon. The sergeant answered in the affirmative. This was a master stroke on the part of the Crown, but much of its effect was destroyed by Macdonagh's cross-examination of the sergeant, which was directed to showing that the latter had prepared the concealment of the money and the weapon in a manner so careful that it was most unlikely that the prisoner could have done so in the short time available to him at the scene of the crime.

Macdonagh fought to the bitter end in the third trial and in his reply for the Crown, Serjeant Armstrong, it was thought at the time, departed from all precedent in the way in which he pressed for a conviction, pouring forth against Montgomery a tornado of contemptuous mockery and denunciation.

Mr. Justice Barry charged the jury quietly and impartially, and they retired to consider their verdict. Within an hour, they had returned, and the issue paper which was handed by the foreman to the Clerk of the Crown bore the word "guilty." When the judge asked Montgomery whether he wished to say anything before sentence was passed, the prisoner thanked him for his conduct of the case, and went on to say that while he had struck the fatal blow, his mind had been unhinged and that he was wholly irresponsible at the time when he had killed his friend Glass.

The issue of insanity had never been raised by the defence during the course of the three trials, and the judge proceeded to pronounce sentence of death. Montgomery was hanged at Omagh gaol, though it was considered that if he had not made his final statement from the dock, the sentence might have been respited.

Not the least interesting feature of the Newtown-Stewart case lay in the fact that counsel on either side, Macdonagh and Armstrong, were rivals both at the Bar and in politics. Armstrong had originally been a Conservative but, changing his party, he won the borough of Sligo from Macdonagh in 1865. If he had remained a Tory, the unexpected advent of a Conservative administration would have placed judicial preferment in his way. As it was, he remained at the Bar. In 1868, an election petition after Armstrong was unseated found both Macdonagh and himself guilty of a degree of corruption which resulted in Sligo being disfranchised for a number of years.

Armstrong was a powerful speaker. To him is attributed the incident where, in the course of cross-examining a handwriting expert, he asked him, " What about the dog?" On the witness expressing his ignorance of the animal in question, Armstrong said, " What about the dog that Baron Dowse said he would not hang on your evidence?" His description of Mitchell Henry, M.P., as " a platter-faced voluptuary " is a good example of his robust style in court.

.   .   .   .   .   .

At Westminster, Gladstone was proceeding with his university bill, which he introduced in the middle of February, 1873. His scheme was an ambitious one. It involved setting up a new university for Ireland, which was to have general control over higher education. The University of Dublin, detached from Trinity College, was to form the basis of this new body, which was to embrace that college itself, the Catholic University, two of the Queen's Colleges (Galway being suppressed), and Magee College, Londonderry. This was to be an undenominational university, both teaching and examining, and was to provide the final solution to the problem of Irish higher learning. So that its education might be purely secular, modern history and philosophy were to be excluded from its teaching.

Palles was entirely opposed to this arrangement. Giving evidence before the Royal Commission on University Education, in 1901, he recalled that although he had been a member of the Government, his views were not accepted :

" The advice of those who knew the views of Roman Catholics of that day, who realised how fully they were convinced of the justice of their claims . . ," he said, " was disregarded."

The popular reactions to the plan were also hostile. The bishops, under the direction of Cardinal Cullen, met and condemned the project as " Godless," stating with a certain amount of truth that it was unjust to endow three of the institutions and leave the Catholic University without any subvention. The Presbyterians were opposed to any scheme that would alter the character of Magee College. The leading men of Trinity College added their condemnation to the scheme. Only eleven of more than a hundred Irish members supported the bill, and on 12th March, 1873, it was defeated in the Commons by three votes, forty-three Liberals voting against it.

Gladstone, who had made the issue one of confidence, resigned from office, but since Disraeli declined to form a Government with a minority, the Liberals returned to office later in the month. They did so, however, in a weakened condition, and for the remainder of his term, Gladstone looked on his Irish supporters with suspicion. He felt that he had, in a sense, been betrayed by them on this important national question, and it is indicative of his imperfect knowledge of Irish affairs at that time that he failed to perceive the defects in his proposed university plan.

At the time the Irish universities bill was before the Commons, a measure was being introduced in the Lords which was also to affect the fortunes of the future Lord Chief Baron in an unforeseen way. This was the Judicature bill. For a long time, it had been felt in England that the system whereby the law was administered in separate courts militated against the successful working of them all. It was therefore proposed to bring together the legal and equitable jurisdictions of these tribunals into one Supreme Court of Judicature; to effect such changes as might be necessary for producing cheapness, simplicity and uniformity of procedure ; and for improving the existing courts of appeal. In addition, the appellate jurisdiction of the House of Lords was to be abolished, and transferred to the new Court of Appeal.

Appeals from Ireland and Scotland were also to go to this new Court, but this point was later abandoned. No immediate steps were taken to carry through similar reforms in Ireland, though in the Commons Gladstone expressed the view that such a change might take place in the near future. In particular, the alleged extravagance of the Irish judicial establishment came under criticism from the Government side of the House, and later in the year Gladstone was understood to have given some sort of undertaking to make economies there.

Three days before Christmas came the decisive event in the legal career of Christopher Palles. On 22nd December, Chief Baron Pigot died, having presided over the Court of Exchequer since 1846.

In the past, it had been customary for the senior Law Officer to receive the offer of a judicial vacancy, and if it had not been for the abnormal political conditions prevailing, Palles would have been appointed as a matter of course. Unfortunately, the issue was complicated by a number of factors. On 27th December, the *Freeman's Journal*, while believing that Palles would be selected, stated that speculation as to the identity of the new Chief Baron was acute. It rejected the notion that the office should be abolished, on the ground that " Ireland derives a benefit only from the judiciary."

Throughout the Christmas vacation, there was a complete silence. When term began on 11th January, nothing had been done to fill the place. Then, on 24th January, in an address to the electors of Greenwich, Gladstone announced the impending dissolution of his administration. It looked very much as if the Liberals would quit office leaving the appointment to their successors. In such a case, Disraeli's choice must naturally fall on Michael Morris, that *rara avis*, a Catholic Conservative. It was rumoured, indeed, that he had already received congratulations on his elevation.

While one cannot be certain, it is possible to hazard a guess as to the reasons for Gladstone's reluctance to appoint Palles. In the first place, he was, as has been seen, profoundly disappointed with the Irish who had deserted him over his universities scheme. Palles, he knew, was a close friend of Cullen, who had attacked it and, in addition, Palles himself had voiced his disapproval. Secondly, Gladstone's experiences a short time before in connection with an English judicial appointment had taught him to avoid such matters if he possibly could do so. In the winter of 1871-72, legislation had been passed to provide for four paid members of the Judicial Committee of the Privy Council. These were to consist of two Indian judges, and two judges of the superior Courts. The English Law Officers were not mentioned ; and the inference was drawn that not only was judicial experience to be a pre-requisite for the appointment, but also that the new Court was not to be made an excuse for political appointments, and to provide rewards for parliamentary supporters. When Gladstone came to make the appointments under the new Act, the Attorney-General, Sir Robert Collier, was designated for one of the places. To qualify him legally for the post, he was appointed a judge of the Court of Common Pleas for two days, and then translated.

The result was an immediate public outcry. Chief Justice Cockburn addressed a protest to the Government, and the subsequent correspondence appeared in the newspapers. The arguments used by the Chief Justice were unanswerable; and the fact that Gladstone affected to understand the protest as being made against the appointment of his Attorney-General to a seat in the Common Pleas was, to say the least of it, unconvincing. In these circumstances, when he came to consider the claims of Palles, it was only natural that he should pause, lest another storm might burst upon him.

At last, the silence was broken. On Tuesday, 17th February, the Dublin newspapers carried a short announcement to the effect that Palles had been offered the post on the previous day and had accepted it. That day, Gladstone went to Windsor and surrendered his seals of office, and the Queen sent for Disraeli. Christopher Palles had been appointed last Lord Chief Baron of the Court of Exchequer in Ireland—with twelve hours to spare.

The conclusion to be drawn is irresistible. Gladstone had changed his mind or rather, he had made up his mind. Somehow or other, pressure must have been brought to bear upon him to appoint Palles. The source of that pressure is most likely to be found in the person of the Chief Secretary, Hartington. Palles and Hartington had worked together for nearly four years, and the Chief Secretary had shared the Attorney-General's dislike of the universities bill. In the proceedings arising out of the Phoenix Park riots, Palles had been leading counsel for Hartington; and on numerous occasions the exigencies of politics had thrown them together. Even their respective rooms in Dublin Castle adjoined each other. What could be more natural than that Hartington should try to do some service for his friend before he too laid down his charge? Amongst Palles's private papers there survives a letter in Hartington's hand, and dated 16th February, 1874, the very day of the appointment. It was addressed from the Irish Office in Great Queen Street, indicating that the writer was in London, and close to the Prime Minister:

" My dear Attorney-General,
 I am sincerely glad to be able to congratulate you on your promotion, to which, as you know, I have always thought that your efficient and loyal services to the Government fully entitled you. I am also convinced that the Government could have made no appointment which could have done them greater credit, or been of equal advantage in the interests of the public. I only regret that there should have been so much delay about it, and that you should have had so much anxiety and doubt on the subject. . . ."

Hartington seems to have been joined in his representations by the outgoing Lord Chancellor, Lord O'Hagan, who took the point that since the vacancy had occurred during his regime, it should be filled on his nomination.

The position of the Irish Chancellor in regard to Irish judicial appointments is somewhat obscure, but it does appear that while he did not have a decisive voice, as his English equivalent has in High Court appointments, his opinion in the matter was entitled to weighty consideration. The decisive factor, however, seems to have been the Chief Secretary's intervention.

In one of the Chief Baron's unreported charges to a criminal jury, there appears this passage:

> "Counsel has said that circumstantial evidence is like a chain depending on its weakest link. I do not agree. Circumstantial evidence is the coincidence of a number of facts, each perhaps weak in itself, but twisted in with the others like strands in a rope, all support and sustain one another until the whole is strong enough to bear the burden of proof."

This is a very apt description of the state of the evidence on the events leading up to his own appointment.

There is an apocryphal story, long current in Irish legal circles and probably originated by Tim Healy, that Gladstone appointed Palles on the railway platform of Paddington station, when on his way to Windsor to resign. Closer investigation, alas, reveals that on Tuesday, 17th February, 1874, Gladstone *did* go to Windsor, but he departed by the 12.45 p.m. train on the London and South Western line, from Waterloo, returning by the 4.15 p.m. from Windsor. On that day Palles was in Dublin. According to the Healy version of the story, Gladstone when about to board the train, was confronted by Hartington who importuned him to sign the instrument of appointment. Though the *Irish Times* stated that the appointment was made on Monday evening, Hartington was in full possession of the facts on the evening of the 17th. One would like to believe that there is some foundation for the legend, but the evidence is against it.

Commenting on the delay in filling the vacancy, *The Times* observed that if it had not occurred, the only objection raised to the new Chief Baron would have been "as to his qualifications or his claims". It is ironic to record that almost forty-six years later to the day, the same news-paper was to chronicle the death of Palles in an obituary which, beginning with the words

> "a long, eminent and honourable life, devoted to the betterment of social institutions and to the elucidation and clarifying of our legal system had been closed",

went on to treat of the Chief Baron in terms of respect and reverence that can seldom have been surpassed in that august journal.

In Ireland, there were no such misgivings, and the *Irish Times* believed that " the whole Bar of Ireland will acknowledge that the position has been honourably earned and worthily bestowed." The appointment was, indeed, a popular one; but it can scarcely have given greater pleasure to anyone than it did to the recipient's father, Andrew Palles, who saw in his son's success his own vindication

Little more remains to be said. On Thursday, the new Chief Baron appeared in the Four Courts, and " although anxious to attract as little attention as possible," he received the public congratulation of his brethren at the Bar. Next day, the letters patent for his appointment reached the Hanaper Office in Dublin, and on Saturday morning, he attended at Lord O'Hagan's house in Rutland Square to be sworn in. Two hours later, O'Hagan himself sat in court to receive the farewells of the profession, voiced by the Solicitor-General. By Tuesday, Palles was hearing chamber motions in the *Nisi Prius* Court, and the longest judicial reign in the history of the common law in Ireland had begun.

X

THE YOUNGEST JUDGE

THE new Lord Chief Baron of Her Majesty's Court of Exchequer in Ireland who took his seat upon the Bench on Tuesday, 25th February, 1874, was a little over forty-two years of age. He was the youngest Irish judge since Tudor times, his brethren being many years his senior. Whiteside, Chief Justice of the Queen's Bench, was sixty-eight; Monahan, Chief of the Common Pleas, was seventy-two; while of the junior Barons of the Exchequer, Francis FitzGerald was sixty-eight, Rickard Deasy was sixty-two, and Dowse was fifty. Even the incoming Solicitor-General, Henry Ormsby, was three years older than Palles, and it was not until the very year of his death that a younger man was elevated to the Irish Bench, when William Evelyn Wylie was appointed to the High Court in November, 1920.

Before examining the judicial scene upon which the new Chief Baron had emerged, it may be instructive to survey the fabric of the stately building that housed the Irish judiciary in 1874, for the Four Courts had by now reached the final form which it was to retain until its destruction in June, 1922.

A visitor entering the Four Courts in the 1870s would have noticed but little change from the elegant vista of today. A stone-flagged floor existed instead of the more modern and more silent covering. Of the six statues which ultimately stood in the Hall, two, Sir Michael O'Loghlen and Chief Baron Joy, were already in place. O'Loghlen had been commemorated by members of the Bar as the first Catholic to hold judicial office since 1688, while the Dean and Chapter of St. Patrick's Cathedral had presented the statue of Joy to the Benchers in 1865.

Off the great central Hall, the four courts themselves opened. Reading clockwise from the entrance lobby, they

were the Exchequer, the Court of Chancery, the Common
Pleas, and the Queen's Bench, and so when Palles was
first appointed he took his seat in the old Exchequer
courtroom.

In earlier times, no library accommodation was provided
for the Bar, and the Hall itself served both as a library
and a consultation room. A gloomy cellar (occasionally
subject to flooding) did duty as a robing room, and all day
long the Hall was thronged with counsel, attorneys, clients,
witnesses, and onlookers. Readers of the works of Richard
Lalor Shiel will recall the animated scenes in the Hall
which he describes, scenes in which O'Connell, Bushe,
O'Loghlen and Joy play a prominent part. For the seeker
after the latest news the Hall had a magnetic attraction
and, in truth, the place of justice had in the mid-nineteenth
century become a fashionable promenade. In 1796, the
Benchers had appointed tipstaves to keep the Hall in an
orderly state, " and free from improper and ill-disposed
persons." A minute of 1852 indicates that the Dublin
Shoeblacks' Society had applied for permission for one of
their number to stand in the Hall for the purpose of black-
ing the boots of Bench and Bar alike. In 1854 leave was
given to one, Margaret Heffernan, " to have a stand for the
sale of oysters in the yard;" and in 1886 it was determined
that " no tables be allowed in the Hall of the Four Courts
for the sale of eatables." In 1867, however, an exception
was made in the case of one, Mary Sullivan, who, on the
recommendation of Master Litton, " was permitted to
have a cake and fruit stand outside the entrance to the
Masters' offices."

The Rolls Court originally occupied the space on which
the Supreme Court now stands, but, in 1835, this was taken
away, and a new Rolls Court and Nisi Prius Court were
built, a little to the right and left of the original site. Later,
a staircase was added at this point, giving access to what is
still called by the more senior members of the Bar "the
old Library." This Library was enlarged to its final
dimensions about 1836, the expense being borne by the
Benchers.

The great Hall was also used for more formal purposes. At the opening of Easter Term each year, the Lord Chancellor held a levee. On the morning of that day, the Bar in robes called on the Chancellor at his home and made their obeisance to him in his drawingroom. There followed a state drive to the Four Courts of the Chancellor and all the judges, in full ceremonial robes, each in his own carriage and pair. Sir John Ross recalled that he was often embarrassed on these occasions by his coachman who, despising his judicial superiors, would land him prematurely at the entrance to the Four Courts.

When the Lord Chancellor's carriage stopped at the front entrance, he entered the Hall, preceded by two tipstaves and the mace bearer and followed by his train bearer and purse bearer, and took his place opposite the main doorway. The other judges entered in their order, and took up their stations, having passed before the Chancellor in order of precedence. The Chancellor then led a procession to the Benchers' room at the rear of the building, where the " customary meeting " was held.

Down to the beginning of the present century, two applewomen had their stands under the clock, and until about 1880, the centre of the Hall was occupied by a rather angular figure of Truth, holding aloft a gaselier. This was always the object of witty allusions, and, in the 1880s, Truth departed to the gardens of King's Inns, where she still stands to delight the children of Dublin. It is sad to record that the restoration of the building carried out in 1928-31 has failed to preserve the spirit of the old Four Courts. No longer do Punishment, Eloquence, Mercy, Prudence, Law, Wisdom, Justice and Liberty look down upon the Hall below them. The judges of today perform their functions unaided by those distinguished legislators, Moses, Lycurgus, Solon, Numa, Alfred, Confucius, Manco-Capac and Ollamh Fodhla, who appeared on the medallions around the dome. Only the panels in the vestibule still survive, bearing their mace and staff, fasces, axe and scales of justice. On the portico, a rather battered Moses, flanked by an excoriated Justice and Mercy and a sedentary Wisdom and Authority, still surveys the Dublin scene. Within, where the glory and pomp have departed, justice is administered with a utilitarian if drab efficiency.

When Palles took his seat on the Bench, it seemed only a matter of time before the judicial reforms projected for England had their counterpart in Ireland. The new Government, indeed, signified its intention to review the position by leaving the Irish Chancellorship vacant, appointing instead a commission, consisting of Sir Joseph Napier, Mr. Justice Lawson, and Master Brooke, to hold the Great Seal. This arrangement lasted only for a year and, in 1875, Ball, the Attorney-General, was appointed head of the judiciary.

Meanwhile, there was much agitation about the forthcoming Irish Judicature bill. The Lord Justice of Appeal in Chancery, Jonathan Christian, had entered the lists with a series of pamphlets, published between 1872 and 1874, in which he criticised freely the proposed settlement. Nor did he content himself with an assault on principle; he also saw fit to treat of his judicial colleagues with a frankness which even the modern press would have regarded as exceptional. Resolutely opposed to the fusion of the systems of law and equity, he examined one by one those personages who were likely to occupy places in the new Court of Appeal and, in the result, little was left to the imagination of the reader. As will be seen, Christian was to return to the attack at a later stage, but one of the results of his activities was the withdrawal of the Irish bill.

The junior Barons of the Exchequer, who were to share the Court with Palles during the last four years of its separate existence, were men of considerable distinction. Francis Alexander FitzGerald, a brother of the Bishop of Killaloe, had been in the Court since 1859. At the Bar, his practice had been mainly in Chancery work, but on the Bench, his reputation as a common lawyer was no less impressive. After the passing of the Judicature Act, in 1877, he retained his seat in the new Exchequer Division. In 1882, he resigned for a very unusual reason. When the

Government introduced the Prevention of Crimes bill that year, it was found that it provided for the trial in certain circumstances of serious criminal offences by judges sitting without a jury. On 19th May, 1882, all the Irish judges met and unanimously agreed to transmit to the Lord Lieutenant a resolution to the effect that the imposition on them of this duty would impair public confidence in the administration of justice in Ireland. The clauses were not deleted (though they remained inoperative) for the feeling of Parliament, a fortnight after the Phoenix Park murders, was in their favour. As a result, Baron FitzGerald felt obliged to resign in protest, and he did so at the end of Trinity Term that year.

The other Barons, Rickard Deasy and Richard Dowse, owed their promotion to their espousal of the Liberal cause. Deasy, a native of county Cork, had held that seat for the party, and had been successively Serjeant-at-Law, Solicitor-General and Attorney-General, before being elevated to the Exchequer in 1861. His task in guiding the Landlord and Tenant Act, 1860, through Parliament has given his name immortality in the legal profession, and it seems a pity to reveal that, in fact, the bill was the creature of his predecessor as senior Law Officer, Napier, and was only taken up by the Liberals at a later date.

As a judge, Dowse was disappointing, for he had acquired a reputation for parliamentary wit. His promotion to the Bench in 1872 drew the following eulogy from *Punch*: —

> " For whinever Dick's pate,
>   Shot up from his sate—
> Like the sun in a state of sublimest good humour—
>   The worst prose in the House
>   Sat as still as a mouse,
> And the sleepiest member woke up at the rumour.
>
>   The reporters' long faces
>   Got short'ning like blazes
> At this smiling oasis such sandy stuff afther ;
>   Why even the bobby
>   Snaked in from the lobby,
> And almost destroyed himself shakin' wid laughther."

After the Judicature Act, Dowse continued to sit in the Exchequer until his sudden death in 1890, at Tralee assizes. In court he occasionally provided the element of stark reality. Thus, in 1889, in *Molloy v. Gray,* where the court had to consider the liability of a defendant who, it was alleged, had created a public health nuisance, Dowse adverted to the offending object in these terms : —

> "The history of this sewer is a matter of some importance. It is like most things connected with this country—a subject on which there may be several opinions. Nobody knows the origin of it; but although it cannot have existed from time immemorial, it has existed for a long time. It has been said to belong to the Grand Jury, and I do not think that it would be anything the better for having them as its projectors. . . ."

This directness of expression had its advantages, for it is recorded that in a *habeas corpus* application before the Exchequer, the anxious wife of the prisoner listened with bemused attention to the careful judgment of the Chief Baron, in which he set forth his reasons in law for refusing to restore her husband's liberty. It required the homelier language of Dowse—" I'm afraid that the prisoner will have to stay in gaol "—to remove the perplexity that was manifest on her face.

The period between 1874 and 1877 was largely occupied by the renewed protestations of Lord Justice Christian who, having failed to subdue his colleagues by his pamphleteering campaign, embarked in a fresh assault on the science of law reporting. In 1876, the *Irish Reports* came in for his condemnation. He complained in open Court of having had his judgments misreported, and he countered this slur on his ability by refusing to furnish to the editors any more of his judicial pronouncements. From the Bench, he declaimed that the reports were " utter nonsense," that their pages were filled with " dry, bald, disjointed twaddle," and that " this miserable little pamphlet " was replete with " mischievous delusions." Lord O'Hagan, who sat with him, attempted a moderate remonstrance, but it was in vain. Attack followed attack. The exchanges between the parties increased in volume and venom and by August, 1877, Christian was the subject-matter of a cartoon in the magazine *Zoz*, entitled "The Martyred Christian."

Later in that year he delivered his final assault on the unfortunate reporters. Alleging again that he had been misreported, the Lord Justice went on to make this devastating comment on the whole system : —

> "In the whole vast ocean of printed matter, since the days of Caxton, I venture to say that there could not be found within an equal space such a mass of utterly worthless rubbish as makes the staple of the eleven Equity volumes of the Irish reports."

Christian's conduct formed the basis of parliamentary intervention, but Disraeli preferred to leave him to his own conscience. After the Judicature Act, indeed, he was elevated to the Court of Appeal, but he remained there only a few months, preferring to resign in the face of changes of which he so heartily and vocally disapproved. Despite his love of unseemly controversy, Christian will always be remembered as one of the great masters of Irish equity, and his learning and erudition were equalled only by his desire to see justice done. Never a strong party man, he shared with Palles and with Francis FitzGerald the unusual distinction of being raised to the Irish Bench without having held a seat in Parliament.

During this time, Palles was finding his feet in the Court of Exchequer; and the first opportunity that arose for him to display his legal erudition was not long delayed, a case that came before the Court in 1875.

The Catholic Bishop of Cork, Dr. Delany, had received a number of legacies from a charitably minded testatrix. These included sums of money for the education of missionary priests, and also a sum of money for the celebration of Masses. The Attorney-General moved before the Court of Exchequer, by way of information, contend-

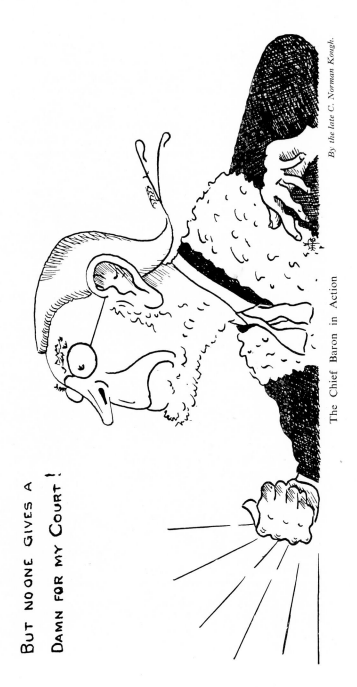

BUT NO ONE GIVES A
DAMN FOR MY COURT!

By the late C. Norman Kough.

The Chief Baron in Action

ing that the legacies were liable to bear legacy duty on the ground that they were not "charitable" in the legal sense.

This was a question of the first importance. In Ireland, unlike England, gifts for Masses had never been regarded as void in law, as being "superstitious;" the question was settled as early as 1823. Their charitable nature was another matter, however. From a fiscal point of view, important exemptions attached to legal "charities," and it was natural that the recipients of such legacies, particularly priests who received Mass stipends, should be anxious to avail themselves of them.

The judgment of the Chief Baron was the first of a series in which he displayed his mastery of this branch of the law. Starting from the assumption that the test of legal charity was one of benefit to the public, he embarked on a most careful analysis of the nature of the Mass itself. After deliberation, he came to the conclusion that in this case, the element of public benefit was lacking, since there was no requirement by the testatrix that the Masses should be celebrated in public. Accordingly, they must bear the legacy duty. He did throw out the suggestion, however, that was to be of prime importance in this branch of the law at a later date, when he said that he thought that such gifts would be charitable if there *had* been such a requirement. In his view, a charitable gift could not derive this element of public benefit from the efficacy, spiritual or temporal, which, according to the beliefs of the donor, the religious service might possess.

Many years later, as will be seen, Palles was to confess his error in *Delany's Case,* and to hold that gifts for Masses, irrespective of the place of celebration, are charitable in Irish law.

A third Judicature bill was introduced in the Commons early in 1877, and after a series of debates, as one writer put it, " on the question how much work could be got out of the Irish judges for how little money," it was passed into law, coming into force on 1st January, 1878. Irish judicial salaries, indeed, were, in the words of Lord Cairns,

" arranged in such a manner that it would have been impossible for human ingenuity to have devised any other scheme which would have secured that no two of them should be equal."

On his appointment, Palles was in receipt of the rather odd sum of £4,612 18s. 8d. per annum, while the Chief Justice of the Queen's Bench had £5,704 9s. 4d., and the Master of the Rolls had to be content with £3,969 4s. 8d. The new Act standardised these salaries, the Chief Baron receiving £4,600 per annum, together with an allowance of £300 for the two circuits each year. These were princely salaries, but they were surpassed by that of the Lord Chancellor, who had enjoyed an income of £10,000 down to 1832, when it was reduced to a mere £8,000.

The reorganisation produced a union of the six Courts of Chancery, Queen's Bench, Common Pleas, Exchequer, Matrimonial Causes and Landed Estates, and transferred their functions to the new Supreme Court of Judicature, consisting of two divisions, a High Court and a Court of Appeal. For the convenience of business, divisions corresponding to the old Courts were retained in the High Court. On the retirement of Chief Justice May, in 1887, the Common Pleas Division was merged in the Queen's Bench, Chief Justice Morris being transferred to the latter division as Lord Chief Justice of Ireland.

The Court of Admiralty was not immediately abolished, but it was to become extinct after the death or resignation of the existing judge. In the event, John FitzHenry Townshend, who had been appointed to the Court, in 1867, held office until 1893. The Court of Bankruptcy was also left out of the scheme, and it was not until 1897, the year in which the Exchequer Division was abolished, that the transfer of Walter Boyd to the Queen's Bench Division ended the separate bankruptcy jurisdiction. At the same time, the death of Robert Warren enabled the Probate Division to be merged.

Under the 1897 settlement, Palles proposed to surrender his independence and to serve as second judge to the Queen's Bench Division, while retaining his precedence after the Lord Chief Justice. When the bill was introduced in the Commons, some of the Irish members proposed an amendment, whereby the Lord Chief Justice, Peter O'Brien, would yield place to the Chief Baron, but the Chief Secretary, Gerald Balfour, told the House that this had been settled by the consent of Palles, and that he himself had drafted the clause which gave precedence to his former pupil.

Palles survived on the Bench for nineteen years after the abolition of his beloved Exchequer. By then he was truly the last of the Barons, for Dowse had died in 1890, and Kelly, the last English Chief Baron, had gone a decade earlier.

In order to complete the picture of the machinery of Irish justice, when Palles was appointed, a word must be said about the staffing arrangements of the Courts.

Originally, the Court of Exchequer was extremely complicated, having a common law side, an equity side, and a revenue side. Moreover, though the revenue side had only an archaic connection with financial administration, the *custodiam* process, which was really a method for the recovery of Crown debts, was frequently made available to private subjects through a legal fiction. In 1819, it appears, the staff of the Court was sixty-nine, but a number of commissions of enquiry in the nineteenth century reduced the system to some semblance of order.

In 1844, a statute was passed abolishing all offices attached to the Courts, with compensation for the holders, and providing for a new establishment. In 1867, a fusion was effected in each office of the pleading and record department. The clerks were divided into three classes and were to be appointed by the two Chief Justices and the Chief Baron, vacancies in the first two classes being filled by promotion. The Judicature Act empowered the heads of the Divisions to define and distribute duties, and " all junior clerkships were to be filled by open competition." All officers attached to a judge, however, were to continue to be appointed by him, and the patronage of the heads of the Divisions was preserved. As a result, the open competition provisions became a dead letter; and it was not until 1904 that anyone was in fact appointed in this way. The dynastic principle was in full operation. Thus, when Palles was appointed, in 1874, one of the first-class clerks in the Exchequer, Henry Yeo, had been appointed in 1829. His son, Henry Vivian Yeo, succeeded to his place in 1879, and remained with Palles until the latter retired in 1916.

XI

" JUSTICE BETWEEN MAN AND MAN "

THE introduction of the new judicial system in Ireland in 1878 imposed additional burdens upon the Chief Baron. Now, apart from his work as the head of his own Exchequer Division, he became a judge of the new Court of Appeal. With the Lord Chancellor, the Master of the Rolls, and the new Lords Justices, Deasy and FitzGibbon, he sat in the tribunal of final resort in Ireland, subject only to the jurisdiction of the House of Lords. One result of this was that Palles, no longer confined to the Exchequer, could now bring his great powers to bear on the branch of jurisprudence which he had made his own—Equity. In addition, his experience at the Bar, coupled with his having to sit in the Court for Crown Cases Reserved, revealed that he was also a master of the principles of the criminal law. He was soon to put this knowledge to good account.

This is not a political history of Ireland in the nineteenth century, but it is inevitable that any study of a prominent judicial personage must take into account the significant happenings of the day. It is also true to say that as man is a victim of his destiny, so the course of political and social events in Ireland during the years between 1880 and 1890 played a vital part in creating for Palles a unique place in the administration of justice.

The nature of the happenings in that decade was such that the law and its administration was brought into the greatest notoriety. The beginning of the period, with the formation of the Land League; the abortive prosecution of Parnell and his associates for conspiracy in 1881; the " Invincible " murder conspiracy; the agrarian tumults of 1886-1890, and the " Plan of Campaign;" all these things had the effect of expressing a great political and economic upheaval in terms of legal administration.

On the one hand, the forces of the Crown, armed with such powers as were deemed necessary by the Government for the preservation of the peace, kept up a relentless pressure on all those who sought to obstruct by force or intimidation the due execution of legal processes. Against them, the skill and acumen of the legal advisers of the Irish party and the Land League were marshalled with the object of setting the plans of the Crown prosecutors to naught. In such a clash of interests, it was inevitable that charges and counter-charges should be levelled against certain members of the Bench. The Irish system, whereby judicial preferment was offered as a reward for political steadfastness (unhappily, still with us), created a situation in which such charges might not be entirely baseless. The names of men like William O'Brien, Q.C., and James Murphy, Q.C., the great prosecuting team, and of Peter O'Brien, Q.C., whose proclivities in the selection of juries have become proverbial, are seldom mentioned even now by lawyers without an uneasy feeling that, perhaps, there may have been some foundation for the strictures of their opponents.

One thing is certain beyond fear of contradiction. Throughout the whole of this troubled period no apologist on either side ever attributed to Christopher Palles any such stigma. At a time when the common law in Ireland might have fallen back into the disrepute in which it had been held in earlier days, the Chief Baron was the one outstanding individual who elevated it above party and polity. His force of character, his integrity and his sense of fairness, these were the qualities he brought to bear on the vexed issues coming before him. " Between man and man," to use his favourite phrase, Palles was determined to do absolute and impartial justice to every party, but above all, he was determined to do it according to law. He had an infinite faith in the common law, and in its adequacy, if properly set in motion, to establish every right and to remedy every wrong. A fragment of one of his jury charges which survives illustrates this:—

"You first have to ascertain the facts. When these are
ascertained, if all the facts are consistent with guilt there
is evidence of guilt. If one certain fact is not reasonably
consistent with anything else, there is proof of guilt."

Whether it was a peasant who resisted the process of
the Court, or a Minister of the Crown who refused to
execute the Queen's writs, the Chief Baron was the stern
vindicator to either. At the same time, his love for legal
forms by no means implies that he was deaf to considera-
tions of natural justice and fair play. On the contrary,
where he found a man a stickler for his legal rights, without regard to the real justice of the case, Palles would find
means within the law to bring him to a sense of fair and
honourable dealing "as between man and man." The
profound respect in which all parties, creeds and classes
of the Irish people held his name was largely due to the
manifest impartiality with which he held the scales between
the Crown and the prisoner. Defended or undefended,
in his hands the latter was assured of justice—rigid as to
evidence, technical as to form, Palles allowed no latitude
to Crown advocacy. His mind inclined towards a strict
observance of the law. No judge could administer it with
greater severity when the occasion arose. No prisoner,
however flimsy his defence, was ever more certain of protection in his life and liberty than when tried before the
Chief Baron.

It is not too much to say that during the period of the
"land war," the Exchequer became a sort of permanent
court of gaol delivery. William O'Brien, James Murphy,
Peter O'Brien, John Naish, Edward Carson and John Ross,
were ranged against D. B. Sullivan, Dick Adams, Tim
Healy, Thomas O'Shaughnessy, Samuel Walker and The
MacDermot. Holding the ring was the Chief Baron. He
always used to say that "We should be supremely grateful
to those Normans, who introduced us to the common
law;" and, with him, the common law was an instrument
in the hand of a master. As Ross put it,

" He would admit no excuse for a slip or error; if he could find any technical flaw in the proceedings, the conviction was quashed and the prisoners went home rejoicing."

Of the mass of litigation handled by him during the period, it is difficult to select cases which illustrate this pervading sense of justice which Palles possessed. Two stand out, however, not only because of their unusual facts, but also because of the way in which he dealt with them.

During the period after the Kilmainham Treaty of 1882, the political agitation in Ireland was directed into constitutional channels. The supposed imminence of Home Rule had stayed the hands of the more violent elements, though even before the defeat of that measure, resistance to eviction had broken out on a number of estates. This was particularly true of the notorious Clanricarde estate in county Galway, whose owner had for long displayed extreme views as to the rights of property owners. A postcard dispatched to the land agent, who had remonstrated with him as to the injustice of an eviction, wherein he had indicated that the agent must not think that his tenants could intimidate him by murdering the former, was characteristic of his attitude.

With the defeat of the Home Rule bill, in 1886, the National League lost no time in producing its " Plan of Campaign," which embodied a new idea for dealing with rack-renting landlords. Tenants on each estate were to decide amongst themselves the abatement of rent they would demand; should that abatement be refused, the rent tendered was to be handed over to a managing committee elected by the tenants themselves and used for the benefit of the evicted.

The estates on which the Plan was put into operation were few; but the Clanricarde estate was an obvious choice, and in October and November, 1886, the rents were collected by the committee organised by the League. Earlier, efforts made by the landlord to execute orders for eviction at Woodford, county Galway, had been unsuccessful, and in August the evictions had been accompanied by scenes of great disorder and bloodshed. The disorder, it seems, was accentuated by reason of the fact that the new Chief Secretary, Sir Michael Hicks-Beach, had decided that a policy of appeasement in the matter of evictions should be followed, with the consequence that inadequate constabulary and military forces were available. Moreover, the forces present were under orders not to assist the bailiffs save in an extremity.

As a result, five men were charged with riot and conspiracy to obstruct the sheriff and his officers, and were returned for trial at the Connaught Winter Assizes, the venue being laid at Sligo. The Chief Baron was the going judge of assize.

From the outset, the affair was an extremely unsatisfactory one. Peter O'Brien led for the Crown, while the defence was conducted by Matthias Bodkin. Strenuous objection was taken to the jury panel, having regard to the religious persuasions of the inhabitants of Sligo, for when it was called over, it was found that it contained 128 Protestants and 122 Catholics. When the assize 'was opened, the panel was impeached, the Chief Baron declaring that it was improperly constituted. " It was impossible to say," he declared, " that any man in the panel had any legal right to be there." This resulted in an adjournment for a new panel.

Meanwhile, Sergeant O'Brien had not been idle. The charges of felony against the prisoners were withdrawn, thus reducing the number of challenges open to them, and there followed a whole month spent in calling over panels, challenging jurors, and other dilatory tactics. An account of these fantastic proceedings was printed in the *Pall Mall Gazette*, from which it appears that, in all, the Crown " stood by " 96 jurors, while the defence challenged 36. Time and time again, Palles intervened to comment on some illegality. He stated that " if he had any discretion with regard to quashing the panel on the ground of irregularity he would have done so;" he forced O'Brien into accepting an adjournment while counsel was assigned to one of the prisoners; and he manifested his profound distaste for the prosecutions and the manner in which they were being conducted.

After many more delays the jury brought in verdicts of guilty against the prisoners, and the Chief Baron put them back for sentence. In the course of the trials, evidence had been given to the effect that during the riots, the police had pursued a policy of non-intervention, and that they had done so under instructions from Dublin Castle.

On 5th January, 1887, the prisoners came up for sentence, and Palles took the opportunity to refer to the conduct of the police in terms that can seldom have been equalled in a court of law. He said:

" . . . . .When facts are proved before me, which show that the public peace in one of the counties over which my commission extends is in grievous peril, and that that peril arises from that which I conceive to be a misapprehension on the part of the officials charged with the preservation of the public peace of the duties imposed on them by common law, by statute, and by their oath of office, I feel that I should not be performing my duty if I did not, with such authority as is afforded by the position which I occupy, state what I conceive to be the law upon the subject. To me it is immaterial what is the rank or station enjoyed by the officials at whom my observations point. I represent the High Court of Justice, and that Court would be useless in this kingdom if it were not entitled to appeal confidently to the authority which the Constitution has given in relation to the execution of its judgments and decrees."

He then went on to describe in detail the happenings at Woodford in the previous August, and said that : —

" For one whole hour breaches of the peace, in gross and open violation of the law, in contempt of the authority of the Queen and of her mandate to the sheriff, were persisted in, in the presence of a strong force of constabulary, and they did nothing."

Speaking of the County Inspectors and Resident Magistrates present at the scene of the evictions, Palles said that his remarks were made on the hypothesis that they had been acting without orders and on their own responsibility. If on the other hand, they had been under orders, he did not wish to make any personal reflection on them:

> "But I take leave to say that in point of law, no illegal order, or unconstitutional order, given by an official—be he Inspector-General, or, going higher, even Under-Secretary or Chief Secretary to the Lord Lieutenant—can justify any man in the violation of the law; and how high soever the position of these officials may be, they are bound by our Constitution to obey the law in the same way as the humblest man who walks the streets."

The Chief Baron concluded his observations with an allocution which deserves a notable place amongst the great statements of the principles of our common law:

> " I desire it to be thoroughly understood that the execution of the decrees of the Judiciary in this country does not depend—as it does not, I believe, in any civilised country—upon the will of the Executive who for the moment may happen to be in office. Into the execution of our writs we cannot allow any question of party politics to enter. If the law be wrong, let the law be altered by the Legislature, and the Judges will at the moment carry out that law as altered. They cannot look beyond the law. They cannot, in the administration of that law, contemplate alterations at a future time. From that pronouncement there is an appeal to the highest court in the realm. But when judgment is once given—the judgment of a court of law, acting within the scope of its jurisdiction—it is not competent to any one in this kingdom, I care not how high he may be, to say that a writ regularly issued on foot of that judgment shall not be executed, or to prevent those who by law are bound to aid in its execution from giving that aid and assistance which the Constitution requires."

Since 1887, much has been written on the doctrine of the "separation of powers" in constitutional law, and much judicial time has been occupied in interpreting such phrases as "due process of law" and "equal protection of the laws," in many cases enshrined in paper constitu-

tions. Words like " liberty " and " freedom " have become
the playthings of the constitutional lawyer. But for a clear
and lucid exposition of the problem as it is applied in the
common law of England this statement by Palles deserves
to rank with the most weighty observations of Marshall,
Holmes, and all the other lawyers who have preceded or
followed him.

The public repercussions were considerable. The Conservative Press, as might be expected, pilloried the Chief
Baron. One publication went so far as to suggest that
owing to his speculations on the stock market, he had been
obliged to resort to Clanricarde for financial assistance,
and so was biassed in his favour! For the Government,
there could not have been a stronger condemnation of
what was a thoroughly dishonest policy. The abortive trial
of the League leaders for conspiracy accentuated the difficulties of the administration and in April, 1887, Hicks-
Beach resigned from office on a plea of failing sight.
Certain it is that his administrative vision had suffered a
prior impairment, and his successor, Arthur Balfour, found
himself with a heavy task.

The Woodford eviction cases had an interesting sequel.
Later in the year, it was decided to hold a meeting there
to celebrate the anniversary of the Plan's operation on
the Clanricarde estate. This meeting had been " proclaimed " as illegal by the Government, and it was held in
defiance of the proclamation, the document in question
being burned by William O'Brien, M.P., in the presence
of Wilfred Blunt, an eccentric Englishman who had
espoused the Irish cause. A month later, Blunt was to
address another meeting, and this was also forbidden.

On the day in question, Blunt mounted his platform and
began the meeting. He was advised to desist by the District
Inspector of constabulary and when he refused to do so,
the platform was cleared. In the resulting mêlée, Blunt was
injured. He was arrested, charged, convicted, and sent to
gaol for two months. On his release, he began proceedings
against the District Inspector for assault, and the case
came before the Chief Baron. An impressive battery of

counsel were arrayed on either side, Peter O'Brien and John Atkinson (afterwards Lord Atkinson) being for the defence. After a week at hearing, during which the cross-examination of the plaintiff formed the highlight of the case, Palles charged the jury, pronouncing a severe condemnation of the Plan of Campaign. He opened with a statement which was generally indicative of his views on trial by jury :

> " I know that you will show your consciousness that the basis of true liberty rests, not upon the Executive Government which may happen to be in power, and which must shift with the changing wheel of fortune, but upon that which will never change—the honest judgment of those to whom our Constitution has delegated the solemn trust of determining by their verdict the legality of the action of that Executive, and of keeping them within the limits to which the law restrains them. That, gentlemen, is the proud privilege which you possess, and which I sincerely trust you may never lose."

As a statement of the principle of government under law, this passage can scarcely be equalled but, it is to be feared, it did little to resolve the doubts of the Dublin jurors, who proceeded to disagree. Perhaps they were intimidated by the fact that the Chief Baron, in explaining the law to them, had told them that in England, " constitutional methods, if not better known, are at least more frequently pursued."

Blunt is alleged to have said that " I would have had a verdict but for Peter the Packer;" and who can say that he was wrong?

The other case coming before Palles in this period was of a common type, involving " boycotting," but was rendered unusual because of the character of the prisoners, who were two Catholic priests. They had been convicted before the magistrates of the offence of inciting others to a conspiracy to boycott what was technically known as a " land grabber "—one who had taken a farm from which the tenant had been evicted. The incitement was alleged to have been given in the course of a public meeting at

which the priests had spoken. A writ of *certiorari* to quash
the convictions was brought in the Exchequer. It was
refused by Palles. In doing so, he was obviously moved,
not only by the fact that the prisoners were of a sacred
calling, but also because of the nature of the incitement
which they had offered. In his judgment, one perceives a
profound sorrow, infused with a righteous indignation, that
they should have used their position in the community for
such a lawless purpose:

> " Here we have the anointed priest of God, who from
> his pulpit on Sundays will inculcate upon his parishioners
> the paramount duty of justice and charity to all men,
> irrespective of the mode in which men may have treated
> them—you have this reverend gentleman telling them that
> they ought, by combined action, to boycott O'Connor—
> that they ought to join in those resolutions if they were
> not parties to them already, and that, if they were parties
> to them, they ought to adhere to and act upon them in
> a way they had not done before . . . . "

One can almost feel his indignation, as he enunciated the
words of his judgment. Palles was a devoutly and unosten-
tatiously religious man, with a lifelong and profound belief
in the tenets of the Church of which he was such an orna-
ment. To him, a case like this must have been doubly
detestable. It outraged his sense of justice, and, as he did
not spare the Chief Secretary in his wrath, so the position
of the prisoners here gave them no immunity from his
denunciations.

The Chief Baron was, indeed, the embodiment of justice;
and he could not conceive that any injustice should be
suffered by the most humble of his fellow-men.

XII

MOUNTANVILLE HOUSE

IT is matter of considerable significance that what was
probably the most important landmark in the political
history of Ireland in the last century coincided with the
attainment by Palles of the summit of his judicial career.
Parnell died on 6th October, 1891. Less than eleven
months earlier the publication of Gladstone's famous letter
to Morley, in which the veteran statesman declared his
inability to support Home Rule if Parnell continued in
the leadership of the Irish Party, had an effect which was
both decisive and disruptive. Hitherto, the hostile elements
in the party had stayed their hands, and the ecclesiastical
authorities, while privately condemning the Irish leader,
had refrained from public anathemas. Now, there was
nothing to be gained by the concealment of moral indignation, and the end came quickly. Deserted by the majority
of those who had hitherto supported him, assailed by the
strictures of episcopal disapproval, Parnell soon passed
from the political scene, leaving behind him a party whose
very divisions served to emphasise the fact that the Irish
people had been united on a purely political issue for what
was possibly the last time.

On Christmas Day of 1891, the Chief Baron was sixty
years of age. He had been upon the Exchequer Bench for
over seventeen years, and had weathered the storms of
the turbulent 1880s. Around him sat men who, while some
of them were his peers in age, were many years his junior
in judicial experience. Of all those who had held office
when he was appointed in 1874, only Lord Justice Barry
remained, Chief Justice Morris having been translated to
the House of Lords in 1889. His last pupil before he had
taken silk was now the Lord Chief Justice of Ireland, Sir
Peter O'Brien, Bart., soon to be ennobled as Lord O'Brien

of Kilfenora. Palles, indeed, had always regarded " Peter "
as a youth, and on one occasion, when they were sitting
together, was heard to exclaim: " Oh Peter, Peter, you
never learned that law from me! "

In that time the Chief Baron's life had undergone many
changes. His father had died in 1880. In his declining
years, he gave up practice as a solicitor and devoted the
greater part of his time to an investigation of the Palles
family history. His enthusiasm, alas, was not matched by
his skill, and such papers as survived him throw but little
light on the family's earlier fortunes.

Within a few years, a more serious calamity was to
supervene. Ellen Palles had always been delicate and her
death in 1885 at the early age of forty-seven was not unexpected. The tragedy occasioned by the incurable mental
illness of their only child, Christopher, had the inevitable
effect of saddening her closing years. Now Palles was left
alone, a widower at fifty-four, with a son that needed constant care and attention. It was at this juncture that his
niece, Bessie, came to his aid. A young woman in her
twenties, she joined her uncle's household at a time of
crisis and soon proved herself to be quite capable of
managing the affairs of even a Chief Baron of the Court
of Exchequer.

Shortly after his elevation to the Bench and following
the general trend in Dublin at the time, the Chief Baron
decided to leave the house in Mountjoy Square and move
south of the Liffey. Fashion dictated this move for the
professional classes, and in the late seventies there was a
general exodus towards Merrion Square and, a little later,
to Fitzwilliam Square and the surrounding streets. Palles
chose what must be the longest Georgian street in Dublin.
It is more than half a mile long, and runs straight from
Merrion Square and Lower Mount Street to Fitzwilliam
Place and Lower Leeson Street. Looking up from the
bottom, one glimpses a tantalising view of the Dublin
mountains, and it was right at the top, on the corner of
Fitzwilliam Place and Leeson Street, that the Chief Baron

took up residence in 1879, in the house known as Number 28, Fitzwilliam Place.

Ever since the Union it had been the fashion amongst the Irish judges to live in a style which accorded with their social position. Many of them possessed imposing country seats. Thus, Chief Justice Bushe had an elegant residence at Kilmurry in county Kilkenny; Lord Plunket was to be found at Old Connaught, near Bray; Chief Justice Lefroy built himself a notable house at Carriglass, near Longford; Baron Deasy was at Carysfort House; Chief Justice Doherty lived at St. Helen's, overlooking Dublin bay; and Mr. Justice Crampton was to be found at St. Valerie, on the Dargle. These country houses, many of them near Dublin, afforded retreats for the judiciary during vacation time; and it was not long before the Chief Baron, whose memories of Mount Palles had instilled in him a love of country life, sought a suitable house.

In 1885, he selected Mountanville House, just outside the village of Dundrum, a few miles from the city. This house had had prior associations with the judiciary. Charles Burton, of the Queen's Bench, had lived there between 1820 and 1827. He was an Englishman who had come over to Ireland as a protégé of John Philpot Curran, and who had rapidly come to the forefront in the profession of the law. It has been suggested, indeed, that it was he who first induced Gerald FitzGibbon, father of the illustrious Lord Justice, to go to the Bar, thus laying the foundation of Ireland's most notable legal dynasty. It was thus fitting that Burton should have as one of his successors at Mountanville an even more distinguished lawyer.

Palles soon established himself in his new environment. From the end of the Spring assizes each year until the beginning of the Michaelmas sittings, he was to be found at his country house. In winter he returned to Fitzwilliam Place, but his life became more and more bound up with Dundrum. With the connection afforded by the Dublin and Wicklow railway from the Harcourt Street terminus, he was within half an hour's journey of the city. Normally, he travelled to Dublin by train and took a tramcar to the Four Courts. One of the best surviving likenesses of the Chief Baron, a pencil sketch by John Butler Yeats, was executed on a tram in 1906. The old man, quite oblivious of the fact that the artist was at work, is deeply immersed in the pages of the daily paper, the customary expression of grim resolution on his features.

Mountanville House is a moderately large one, approached by two entrances, each with its attendant gate lodge. A fine entrance porch, supported on Ionic columns, leads into the main hall, filled in the Chief Baron's time with that accumulation of palms, bamboos, and stuffed tropical birds which was the essential adjunct of Victorian decoration. There were some things of beauty, too; a fine portrait of Mary of Modena (second wife of James II), by Lely, and a most attractive portrait of Archbishop Oliver Plunkett, a kinsman of Palles, which still continues in the possession of the family.

The drawing-rooms overlooked a fine terrace, and had a westerly aspect. The main drawing-room, we learn, was decorated in white and gold, and in the hangings and upholstery the predominant tones were pale yellow and green; here, again, palms, ferns and flowering plants were an essential element. The truth is, of course, that the Chief Baron was an extremely enthusiastic gardener. The gardens and hot houses at Mountanville covered over twenty-five acres, and nothing gave their owner greater pleasure than to take a visitor on a tour of his fernery which, it appears, was watered by an ingenious system of pipes devised by himself and his engineer brother, Andrew. An orchid house, vineries, and ranges of peach houses completed this picture, and in the grounds there was a pine walk, circular in form and just a mile around, thickly planted on both sides with firs, pines, copper beeches, laurels and other trees.

As might be expected, the centre of the house was the Chief Baron's study. Here hung a fine portrait of his friend, Lord Justice Barry, and here was to be found a choice collection of books of general interest. He was in the habit of working at a large desk, and there was also

The.Chief Baron —
in a train — Dublin
Oct. 1906 —
J B Yeats

A pencil sketch by John Butler Yeats

an upright writing bureau near the window, where he was wont to write standing, protected from draughts by an ornate tapestry screen. Mountanville was uncontaminated by the influence of the law, however, and the legal work appears to have been confined to the house in Fitzwilliam Place.

Both at the house in the city and at Mountanville were to be seen his really striking characteristic—a deep devotion to his religion. Shortly after he went to Fitzwilliam Place he obtained ecclesiastical sanction for an oratory there, and he made like provision at Dundrum. One who knew him throughout his life has summed matters up by saying that " he was a great Christian gentleman, and the Roman Catholic religion guided every day and every act of his life." All the evidence points to this as being an accurate assessment of one who seems at all times to have had a peculiar awareness of the inner spiritual life. It was commented upon by all who knew him; and there can be no adequate description of his very unusual sanctity.

In this context, Palles was to form a series of friendships with his new neighbours, the Jesuit fathers at Milltown Park, which were to endure for his lifetime. Two members of the Society, in particular, Father Peter Finlay and Father Charles Mulcahy, became his close friends. Father Finlay's acquaintance with him went back to 1866, and on the occasion of his death the priest wrote a notable memoir of his friend and mentor. Father Mulcahy, too, was very close to Palles, beginning his connection with him when he first came over from Milltown to celebrate daily Mass at Mountanville. Later, as a master at Clongowes, Father Mulcahy used to delight his schoolboy listeners with tales of the lively breakfast conversation for which his host was renowned.

In the conduct of his domestic arrangements, the Chief Baron was acutely aware of the dignity due to the head of Her Majesty's Exchequer Division. Even in the last decade of the nineteenth century, there must have been few houses in Ireland in which afternoon tea in the drawing-room involved the services of two footmen, and in which a white tie and tails were the daily attire for family dinner. As one who recalls him observed rather irreverently, " The Chief was very charming, but it was rather like dining with the Pope." Perhaps he was a little pampered. No newspaper damp from the press was allowed to touch his hands, and the papers had to be dried at the fire before he came down to breakfast. He was mothered by his valet, Albert, who used to come in with a rasher on a plate, lean over his master confidentially and murmur, " Y'Lordship's little bacon ".

From all this, it must not be assumed that Palles led the life of an ascetic recluse. On the contrary, he played a leading part in the social life of Dublin. During the years from 1890 down to the outbreak of the first world war in 1914, the outward political stability of Ireland tended towards a more enlightened social sense amongst the ruling classes in society. The judges themselves were men of real substance, and they formed an important unit in Dublin society. Many of them combined their work with extra-judicial attainments. Gerald FitzGibbon, for example, Lord Justice of Appeal for over thirty years, possessed intellectual gifts of a high order. His home at Howth was the meeting place of many notabilities, and Lord Randolph Churchill spent much of his leisure time there. Dodgson Hamilton Madden, a judge of the Queen's Bench Division, who has been described as " a don that had strayed into the Courts," was a Shakespearean scholar of the first rank, and it is sad to think that, today, his book on deeds registration is better known in Ireland than his *Diary of Master William Silence.*

The Lord Chief Justice, who held court at Newlands House, near Clondalkin, was the centre of much judicial conviviality. In his later years Lord O'Brien recalled many of the Christmas parties spent with the FitzGibbons at Howth. On one occasion, he recounted, he had to leave by an early morning train for Dublin. He had not been home very long when a mock warrant for his arrest arrived. It had been sent by FitzGibbon and was worded in the correct legal phraseology to the effect that O'Brien had stolen a boot, the property of the Right Honourable George Wyndham, Chief Secretary for Ireland. In his precipitate departure, he had taken the wrong boot. He had noticed that his footwear was a little tight, but he had attributed this to FitzGibbon's hospitality.

In official circles, too, the great tradition of entertaining had been revived. At the Vice-Regal Lodge, after the austerities of his immediate predecessors, Earl Dudley set a high standard, and this was adopted by the Balfour brothers, John Morley and George Wyndham. In his memoirs, Morley recalled discussions over the dinner-table, when Palles, FitzGibbon, Madden, and Lord Wolseley joined issue on such topics as the morality of suicide, the deterrent effect of capital punishment, and the incidence of perjury among Irishmen. On the Chief Baron's observing on one occasion that "no man with plenty of good hard work ever committed suicide," the reply of "Castlereagh" was immediately forthcoming from Wolseley, the Irish Commander-in-Chief. We also learn from Morley that Palles, in opposition to John Gibson, Chatterton and Madden, was in favour of allowing prisoners to give evidence in criminal cases.

"It really depends," he said, "which maxim you adopt as paramount—anything rather than that an innocent man should suffer, or anything provided a guilty man should be caught."

Another personage who seems to have played a considerable part in Palles's social round was Father Healy, the celebrated parish priest of Little Bray. Thus, on 16th October, 1894, Healy wrote bidding him to "a little dinner" at Ballybrack, to meet "Mr. Morley, Archbishop Walsh, and other celebrities." One is tempted to speculate on the purpose of that dinner party, and one feels that the Chief Secretary went home that evening more fully informed on the question of higher education for Catholics.

It was about this time that the Chief Baron acquired the habit of foreign travel. The Long Vacation was frequently spent at St. Moritz, always in the company of Bessie, his faithful travelling companion. There they met their friends the Ashbournes, the Morrises, and the Wyndhams. In 1894, writing to his brother Andrew, he confessed that the hotel was "rather full", and attributed the popularity of the resort that year to the presence of the Duchess of York.

Some of these letters written from abroad are revealing. While Palles was at St. Moritz in 1892, he received the news that he was to be sworn of the English Privy Council —an almost unprecedented honour for an Irish judge who had never attained the House of Lords. Writing to his niece, Mrs. Dallas Pratt, he confided:

> ". . . Did you hear that they have made me an English Privy Counciller? It was published in *The Times* two days before I heard of it. In England it is considered a great honour. Between ourselves, I don't think much of it, but one likes his existence to be recognised and as I know that it was intended to gratify me I am gratified accordingly. We lunched yesterday with Judge Mathew and his family . . ."

In this fragment we perceive the modesty of the man, allied with his essentially buoyant sense of humour. Honours and distinctions did not interest him, and it was generally known that he had refused a knighthood in the same way as he had twice refused the offer of the Lord Chancellorship. The sudden death of Hugh Law in 1881 had been the occasion of the first offer. Then, he had been content to allow his name to be put in the commission for the great seal. Sir Edward Sullivan's death two years later had brought the second offer, but again Palles refused, preferring to see the office pass to another old Clongownian, John Naish, of the Munster Circuit. Family circumstances necessarily precluded the acceptance of an hereditary honour which had become the usual accompaniment of the Lord Chancellorship, and Palles was content to remain at the Exchequer.

A frequent visitor to St. Moritz during this period was Lord Morris. Morris, who received a life peerage as a Lord of Appeal in Ordinary and who lived to attain an hereditary dignity under the style of Lord Morris and Killanin, had been Chief Justice of the Common Pleas and later Lord Chief Justice of Ireland. He was a close friend of Palles, and the latter frequently stayed with him in London and at his country seat near Spiddal. It is recounted by his biographer that during one of his visits to Switzerland, he was impelled to disparage the fact that Palles—an inveterate reader—had brought with him a trunk filled with "yellow backs," the sensational fiction of the nineties. A mutual taste for conversation ensured that the trunk remained unopened, but one day, while Morris and Palles were leaning over a bridge near their hotel watching the little stream below, the Chief Baron's teeth became dislodged and precipitated themselves into the water.

Overcome by his loss, it is alleged, Palles called upon the *curé* of the village on his way home to report the matter, lest the errant dentures might be recovered by one of his parishioners. The next day, Sunday, the two Irish lawyers attended Mass, and to Palles's acute discomfiture the *curé* preached a sermon on the very distinguished visitor's loss—whom they had with them in church at that very moment—and suggested that the congregation should turn out in the afternoon in order to join in the search.

The Chief Baron returned to his hotel, and sat miserable and embarrassed in his room, angry and perforce silent. "Now is the time for your yellow trash," said Morris soothingly, dragging out the big trunk. "While I am dining, you can devour these."

It was through his assize work that the Chief Baron contracted one of his closest and most enduring friendships, with the Pirrie family in Belfast. He always took his assize work seriously. From 1892 down to 1915, the year he last went out, he never missed a circuit, and in that period he made no fewer than forty-eight journeys through the country. Only once, in 1912 (when he was over eighty), did he miss a sittings through illness, and on that occasion he omitted but one town, Waterford. He was always prepared to take the heaviest circuit, the North-East, with the lengthy sittings at Belfast. Over the years, he presided at the county Antrim Assizes on no fewer than fifteen occasions, his brother judge being either Lord Chief Justice O'Brien, Lord Justice FitzGibbon, or Mr. Justice Johnson; in addition, he frequently took the Winter Assize for " the Ulster Winter Assize County," held at Belfast, but embracing the North-West and North-East circuits.

In 1898, he owed his escape from possible injury to the fact that the Lord Chief Justice was with him, and to the fortuitous circumstance that the Judicature Act of the previous year had placed him junior to the head of the Queen's Bench Division. The latter was the " judge in commission," and a prisoner named Robert Gordon came before him and was convicted of burglary. As soon as O'Brien passed sentence, the prisoner threw a stone at him, and attempted to jump over the rails of the dock. The stone passed just above the judge's head, and rebounded at his feet. The Lord Chief Justice was reported as observing immediately after the occurrence that " it is eminently necessary that a judge should endeavour to show great presence of mind during every portion of his judicial career."

A case which he tried at Downpatrick assizes in the summer of 1898 illustrates Palles's straightforward approach to civil bill appeals from the County Courts. It was an action against the Ballynahinch gas company, for the negligence of their manager in causing an explosion by the rather imprudent practice of looking for an escape of gas with a lighted match. The scene of the occurrence was a barber's shop, and the plaintiffs were seriously injured. They belonged, we are told, " to the labouring class," and they were in the course of being shaved in the shop when the explosion took place.

The Chief Baron had no doubts about the liability of the defendants to pay them damages, for if he held otherwise, he said, " it would be giving everyone liberty to blow up all the shops in Ballynahinch." It had been argued that since the barber's customers were unemployed at the time, they were entitled to very small damages, but he did not agree: " I shall give something in addition to that," he declared, " for I do not think it just that a man should be blown up and then told that all that he is entitled to is a sum equal to the wages he would have earned and the medical expenses he has been put to." As a result, the plaintiffs went away rejoicing, feeling, doubtless, that their sojourn in the barber's establishment had turned out to be a fortunate one.

Palles liked Belfast and the Ulster people and, one suspects, arranged matters so that his judicial visitations there would be frequent. One of his registrars recalls that he would often decide to walk to the court-house in the Crumlin Road on a fine morning. He would take the registrar's arm, and they would parade the streets of Belfast, followed by the empty carriage and a jingling, clattering escort of mounted police.

Through the Pirries, he began to learn more and more of the North of Ireland, knowledge which was to stand him in good stead in his educational work. Through them, too, he developed the habit of transatlantic voyaging which was a feature of his later years.

The first trip to America and Canada was made in the Long Vacation of 1899. The link between Belfast and the United States was a particularly close one in that year, for Sir Thomas Lipton had issued his first challenge for the America's Cup with his yacht, *Shamrock,* from the Royal Ulster Yacht Club. The Chief Baron and his niece, Bessie, both of whom travelled over with the Pirries aboard the *Oceanic,* visited Sandy Hook to witness the first of Lipton's attempts to win the famous Cup.

On this trip, they travelled extensively, visiting Portland, Boston, Rochester, Buffalo, Niagara Falls, and Quebec, where the Chief Baron found it necessary to make a speech. Thence they proceeded to Montreal and Toronto, leaving for Liverpool aboard the *Oceanic* on 18th October. On the return journey they were joined by Admiral Lord Charles and Lady Beresford, en route for home from the China station, and an autographed dinner menu which survives the voyage shows that the White Star Line lived up to its great reputation for passenger comforts.

After the first holiday afloat, few summers passed without a trip to America. The Chief Baron's travelling companion on these subsequent occasions was often the Recorder of Cork, Mathew J. Bourke, K.C. In his delightful recollections of the Munster Circuit, Maurice Healy tells the story of the occasion on which Palles, en route for New York aboard the *Adriatic* with Matt Bourke, was visited at Queenstown by Standish O'Grady, Clerk of the Crown for the county Cork, who deemed it his duty to pay a call on the Chief Baron as he passed the harbour.

By an unfortunate mischance, the moment at which O'Grady began to pay his addresses coincided with his recognition by a female passenger, one of the least strait-laced of the musical comedy stars, who greeted O'Grady with what, for the occasion, must have appeared to be unseemly familiarity, asking him to join her in a drink. The Chief Baron, with a mischievous smile, said: "Come on, O'Grady; present me to the lady; and if you will not accept the invitation, I certainly will."

Once when he had returned from a vacation trip, the Chief was visited by a member of the Bar in his chambers, who took the opportunity of expressing the hope that he had profited by his rest. "I do not like being idle," he said, "I am always working. See, see"—a favourite introductory particle—"did you ever know why a Cambridgeshire labourer doesn't live long? Because he doesn't use his brain—and it rots!" Even when he was on holiday, his mind was seldom far from the law. On a journey in France with Matt Bourke he was discovered brooding over a railway turntable, which was insecurely fenced, and sorrowfully saying, "Ah, Recorder, I'm grieved they haven't heard of *Cooke v. Midland Great Western Railway Company* here!"—a reference to a case on the law of negligence in which he had taken a leading part.

At home, there were visits to Belfast to stay with the Pirries; excursions to London; and, most exciting of all, an invitation to the Coronation of King Edward VII and Queen Alexandra, in August, 1902. Writing to her sister afterwards, Bessie was careful to say that "they gave The Uncle better seats than any of the other Irish judges. Judge Madden was in the south gallery, so also were the Pirries." Bessie described the ceremonies in great detail and with much feeling, observing that

> "The Uncle bore the long wait very well, and the excitement, as everyone was carried away by the event. I would not have missed it for anything and it will be a thing to think of when one is old."

Of the more amusing domestic incidents, the affair of the Chief Baron's portrait is worthy of chronicle. Some time in 1902, it seems, Bessie and the Pirries decided that "The Uncle's" portrait must be painted. Mrs. Pirrie approached the most fashionable artist of the day, Sir Hubert von Herkomer, and suggested that he might interest himself in the commission.

Von Herkomer's reply was a revealing one. The question, he said, was "easily answered—500 guineas is my price for half length portrait, and 600 guineas for ordinary three-quarters." He added that he would most certainly like to assume the task, for "the strong neck and head of the Lord Chief Baron greatly interested me."

The Chief Baron himself was not quite so enthusiastic, and in reply to a letter from von Herkomer, he observed in his usual forthright manner that he would not "like to give more than five hundred guineas for my portrait—whether it is half length or three-quarters." He went on to say:

> "I confess that for years I have had and even still have rather an objection to having my portrait painted. I cannot think that even your great skill can make a decent picture of a battered down old man such as I am. My only reason for now consenting is the great desire of my niece and the fond hope that as you have performed such miracles in portraits you may make something of me."

These objections are understandable, for the old man did not wish to be reminded of that earlier portrait, painted with his wife, Ellen, by his side, on the honeymoon trip to Paris. But the qualms had to be suppressed, and the blandishments of the artist, supported, one imagines, by Bessie's flattery, resulted in a number of sittings in London. There was much discussion about the wearing of his wig and in the end, a compromise was reached by having it placed on the table beside the subject. At length, in June, 1903, the precious portrait was consigned to Dundrum station where, as von Herkomer reminded the Chief Baron, " a word in the station master's ear would work wonders for its safety."

Von Herkomer's likeness of Palles is, on the whole, a faithful one. He caught the power of the head, the prominent nose, the firm mouth, and the kindly eyes. Clad in his scarlet and ermine robes, bare-headed, but wearing the beautiful gold collar of SS of the Chief Baron, Palles is indeed an impressive figure. It is a portrait that repays study. At first it seems superficial, but as one returns to it, one discerns in it a strange fascination, and the dominating influence of a strong personality.

For many years the portrait hung in Mountanville, and after the Chief Baron's death, Bessie kept it with her until she, in turn, passed away. After further wanderings, it came to Glasgow, where by a fortunate accident, the Chief Baron's grand-niece, Mrs. Irma Waddell, made the acquaintance of Provost Alton of Trinity College, and in 1949 she presented it to the College. It now hangs at the top of the staircase leading to the Fellows' Common Room.

There is a copy of von Herkomer's portrait (by an unidentified artist) in King's Inns, where it occupies a place of honour over the fireplace in Hall. In January, 1918, Sir John Ross, then a neighbour and intimate friend of the retired Chief Baron, informed the Benchers that the latter wished to present such a copy to the Inns. The offer was gratefully accepted and the copy was hung in April, 1919.

From the time of his election as a Bencher he had taken

a continual interest in the affairs of the Society, and he scarcely ever missed a meeting of the Bench. His devotion to the Inns as a manifestation of the corporate personality of his profession was characteristic of the man, and it was also inspired, one thinks, by his deep interest in the question of legal education. When the Society of Public Teachers of Law was formed in 1909, one of its earliest actions was to communicate with the Chief Baron, asking him to accept the honorary membership of the Society. His reply is both characteristic and revealing:

10th January, 1910.

My dear Professor Goudy,

I received your two flattering letters a few days since. I am not vain enough to one moment think that I deserve all the kind things you say of me. This however I know, that I have been always anxious even before my call to the Bar that our law should be placed on a more scientific basis than it was then or is now. This I have for many years found by experience must ultimately rest on legal education. And consequently I quite agree with you when in the course of your admirable introductory address, you say that on you, the public teachers of law, undoubtedly rests in considerable measure responsibility for the competence of our future judges . . . and to some extent of our legislatures, statesmen and administrators. Your Society confers upon me a highly esteemed honour by asking me to become one of their Honorary Members and I gratefully accept it. Believe me, my dear Professor,

Very truly yours,

C. Palles.

The other recipients of the honorary membership on that occasion—Sir William Anson, Mr. Justice Holmes, Sir William Markby, Sir Frederick Pollock, Bart., Professor J. B. Ames and Professor Heinrich Brunner—indicate that in the view of the members of the new Society, Palles was a master of his subject. His appreciation of the part played by the law teacher was characteristic of the acuteness of his powers of observation; such expressions of opinion, unusual today, were all but unknown from such a source fifty years ago.

Such were the incidents which lightened the burden of approaching old age. But there was other and more serious work to be done, work outside the scope of his judicial duties, in the field of educational reform generally, and it is to this aspect of Palles's career that we must now turn.

XIII

EDUCATION FOR THE PEOPLE

PREVIOUS assessments of the intellectual qualities of Christopher Palles have laid stress on the fact that, unlike many of his judicial contemporaries, he was preoccupied with his legal work to the exclusion of all other matters. It is true, certainly, that the extraordinary confidence which he engendered in all classes stemmed from the feeling that he represented that single-minded devotion to the principles of the common law which is said to characterise its best exponents: but this is not the whole story. From what has been said already, it will be apparent that he was a man of wide interests; and his seeming reticence was probably derived from a belief that it was unseemly for a member of the Bench to become involved in popular issues.

In one matter, however, the Chief Baron was prepared to take an active part, and that was the question of providing equality of opportunity in education for all his fellow-countrymen. Here he had formulated the most clear-cut and definite views, and here he would admit of no compromise. All the people of Ireland and, in particular, all his co-religionists, he thought, were entitled as of right to enjoy the benefits of the best educational system at every level. In his view, many of the evils which became manifest in the relations between Great Britain and Ireland in the past had proceeded from the educational inequalities which had been visited on the people of the latter island, and he was prepared to do everything consonant with his position to see that these inequalities were removed.

Although he was to reveal in old age that he had been keenly concerned in university reform since his early days at the Bar, his first formal contact with the problem of Irish education came with his appointment as a Commissioner on the Intermediate Board, in 1878. The purpose of this body, some may recall, was to promote secondary education in Ireland, by holding public examinations for pupils, by awarding exhibitions and prizes to successful candidates, and by paying " results fees " to the managers of the schools.

One effect of the legislation was to bring into competition the secondary schools of the different religious denominations, and the statute setting up the Board contained a " conscience clause " similar to that which had been used to resolve the denominational education question in England. It provided, in effect, that no pupil was to be permitted to remain in attendance at a school during the time of any religious instruction which the pupil's parents or guardians had not sanctioned. It is hardly necessary to say that the clause had no effective operation in any Irish school which was strictly denominational. As Palles was to point out later, with respect to his own old school, no matter to what extent religion was involved with secular teaching at Clongowes, the managers were able to make the declaration required by the statute. In the field of primary education, however, this clause was to have implications in the future, mainly through the instrumentality of the Chief Baron himself.

Palles sat on the Intermediate Board for thirty-two years, becoming chairman in 1896 and retaining that position until his resignation in 1910. During that time, he gave his continual attention to the affairs of Irish secondary education. In addition, he was largely concerned with the allied problems of primary education, having been appointed a Commissioner of the National Board in 1890.

At the time of his accession to that Board, the whole topic of Irish primary education had been restored to the realm of popular controversy. The National schools, which dated from 1831, had been set up, as was seen earlier, on the basis of the mixed system. There was, nevertheless, a very considerable demand for separate schools by the various religious denominations in Ireland and, in particular, by the Catholics. By 1880, indeed, no less than half

of all the National schools were being worked on a *de
facto* denominational basis.

The appointment of Dr. Cullen as Catholic Archbishop
of Dublin had resulted in an intensification of this demand.
The other bishops joined in the campaign and, in 1870, a
Royal Commission made a strong recommendation for the
removal of all religious restrictions in schools where the
pupils possessed denominational uniformity. This was not
implemented, however, and Cullen's successors, McCabe
and Walsh, continued to pursue the claim with increasing
vigour.

The existence of the " Model Schools," which were de-
signed as part of the general plan of training primary
teachers and which were under the direction of the
National Board, added to the Catholic grievance. The fact
that the teachers' training colleges themselves were conducted on undenominational lines (and so came under the
ban of the bishops) meant that the vast majority of Irish
primary teachers in the Catholic schools were untrained. It
was not until 1885 that Trevelyan, Gladstone's Chief
Secretary, made provision for the establishment of Catholic
training colleges and, even then, they suffered certain
financial disadvantages. Apart from a small lay minority,
of which Lord O'Hagan was the spokesman, Catholic
opinion as a whole had now turned away from the mixed
system, and pressure for reform grew apace.

For a time the energies of the bishops were, as will be
seen, diverted to the question of university education, but
by 1892, the interest of the Nationalist politicians in the
primary schools had been aroused. In that year the passage
of a school attendance bill through the Commons was
made the occasion of an attempt to introduce a conscience
clause which could be accepted by the denominational
primary schools without breach of principle. The proposer,
Sexton, secured from the Chief Secretary an agreement to
the proposal and an undertaking that he would bring it to
the attention of the National Board. This he proceeded to
do, but before the latter body had had an opportunity of
considering it, Gladstone assumed office at the head of a

Liberal administration on 15th August, 1892, and John Morley took over the Irish Office.

Throughout these negotiations, the most active exponent of the new plan was the Archbishop of Dublin, Dr. Walsh. Since his appointment to the see in 1885, he had been in the forefront of this movement and his close friendship with Palles was manifested at a special meeting of the National Board on 25th October, 1892, when the latter proposed that the regulations be amended in the sense of the Chief Secretary's directive. His motion was carried by a majority of eleven to three, and the regulations then awaited the sanction of the Irish Government.

The proposal was not carried without protest. A number of the diocesan synods of the Church of Ireland deplored the departure from the undenominational principle, and a hostile body of nonconformist opinion was marshalled by T. W. Russell. In addition, it was known that Morley's own views were not sympathetic, though he had earlier expressed his understanding of Archbishop Walsh's point of view. In the event, he refused to sanction the new regulations, giving as a reason that they had not been carried by the Board with " so near an approach to unanimity " as was necessary. The Liberal dependence on the English nonconformist vote was probably a decisive factor in this result. For Palles, this was a bitter disappointment, and he felt keenly the injustice suffered by the denominational schools. Ever tolerant of the views of others, however, he did not allow the affair to mar his relations with Morley, and even after the latter had left Ireland permanently, they kept up a frequent and cordial correspondence.

It was in the sphere of university education, however, that the personality of the Chief Baron had its most determined impact; and both in public and in private, he pressed the claims of the Irish Catholics for a final settlement of the question. It is not too much to say that his influence was a decisive one, and that the pattern of university education as it exists today is due to a large extent to it.

Throughout the nineteenth century the provision of a place of higher education acceptable to Catholics played a sporadic part in Irish politics, and, it will be recalled, it was the non-acceptance of Gladstone's settlement that led to the downfall of his first Government in 1874. From time to time the matter was raised in the House of Commons, though without any satisfactory result. As early as 1866, the Russell ministry had attempted to find a solution by altering the charter of the Queen's University in Ireland by a supplemental charter, enabling candidates to obtain the University's degrees without having attended any of the Queen's Colleges. Hostility to this move, mainly from the Belfast college, resulted in legal proceedings which rendered the new charter ineffective, and matters remained much as before. Stimulus for the plan had come from a motion by an Irish member, The O'Donoghue, for a charter for the Catholic University, and while no more success attended the efforts of Lord Mayo, the Chief Secretary, to obtain concessions from his party in 1867, on the failure of his proposals, the Catholic laity decided to put their own views forward.

The moving spirit behind this scheme was the Right Hon. Richard More O'Ferrall, a kinsman of Palles, who was associated with The O'Conor Don, William Monsell (afterwards Lord Emly), and other prominent Catholic laymen. A public declaration was drawn up to the effect that the signatories felt that there must be a change in the system of university education, and that such change should place Catholics on a basis of parity with their fellow-countrymen. The declaration was signed by a large number of influential Catholics, including Palles himself, and was laid before the Prime Minister in 1870.

Gladstone's efforts at a solution proved abortive and the defeat of his bill brought down his Government. The rise of the Home Rule party had the effect of keeping the matter before the public gaze, however, and in 1879 Disraeli sought yet another solution. He left the three Queen's Colleges, Trinity College, and the University of Dublin unassailed, but his legislation provided for the abolition of the old Queen's University and the substitution of a new body, the Royal University of Ireland. This was empowered to grant degrees to all persons who had passed the prescribed examinations, whether or not they had attended at a university college, the study of medicine being excluded from its purview. It had the advantage that by its establishment, there were provided a series of fellowships, affording an indirect endowment for the Catholic University; and the Catholic population as a whole supported the " Royal."

The return of Gladstone to power in 1880 did not affect Disraeli's plan. Like the Intermediate system in the schools, the new University enabled students of all denominations to compete for its prizes on a basis of equality, and the Catholic University, now taken over by the Jesuits and known from 1882 as "University College, Dublin," afforded a sound training ground for those Catholics who were unwilling to attend Trinity College. The division of control in the Royal University itself between the different denominations led to understandable friction, however, and the official Catholic attitude to the system was that it could be no more than a temporary expedient. Archbishop Walsh continued to press for changes in a series of forthright and lucid pronouncements. The Chief Baron, inhibited by his office, was unable to take any public part in the controversy at this stage, but in giving evidence before the Royal Commission in 1901, he was prepared to say that he had " thought of it " for a long time—certainly since 1887. At all times he seems to have been in the closest collaboration with the Archbishop who, though he refused to testify before the 1901 Commission, stated in his reply to the invitation that " The Lord Chief Baron has said everything that I should wish to say."

In 1890 Walsh published a pamphlet in which he put forward a number of possible plans for a settlement of the question in a manner acceptable to Catholics. The first was one State-aided university, embracing all the existing institutions. The second involved two universities —one, the University of Dublin, enlarged to include a new Catholic college as well as Trinity College, the other a modified Royal University. Finally, he proposed three universities—the University of Dublin as it existed, a new Catholic university with its principal college in Dublin, and a university for nonconformists based on the Queen's College, Belfast. Any of these plans, said Walsh, must involve the public endowment of the Catholic college in Dublin, the re-constitution of the Queen's Colleges at Cork and Galway in order to make them acceptable to Catholics, and adequate Catholic representation on the governing body of the university proposed in his first plan, or of the two proposed in the second, or of the Catholic university envisaged in the final one.

These proposals produced instant and vociferous hostility from the Protestant sections of the community, for each trenched upon the position of one of the Protestant churches.

Further statements from the hierarchy in 1897, and a re-affirmation of the 1870 declaration by the laity, kept the agitation alive, and in 1901, a Royal Commission was set up, under the chairmanship of Lord Robertson, to investigate the whole question, excluding Trinity College. On 17th December, 1901, Palles travelled to London to give evidence before this body.

From the outset it was clear that he had his mind made up as to the correct answer to the whole problem. He thought the existing situation quite unsatisfactory, and productive of rank injustice. The fact that there *was* an adequate system of primary and secondary education for Catholics, the Chief Baron thought, added to the evils of the situation, for it had led to the existence in Ireland of a half-educated class, unfit for any employment, and so "dissatisfied, disaffected, and—I go the length of saying—dangerous to the State." In addition, he asserted, the absence of an acceptable university reduced the standard of training for teachers, and it also inhibited the Crown from appointing Catholics to responsible positions in the public service. When he was asked whether he thought the facilities provided by the Royal University were sufficient, he said:

> "My own view is that it is merely an examining body, and nothing more. I have the old-fashioned idea of a University that I acquired when I was at that venerable institution, Trinity College, of which I am as fond, and which I am as anxious to support, as the eminent Provost of it can be. I learned there that you can have no true University unless it is a teaching body. . . ."

Palles then went on to propound what he called his "ideal solution." It was, in effect, Walsh's second plan, He would like to see founded within the University of Dublin a new college, "which should be as Roman Catholic as Trinity College is Protestant," and he went on to set out in detail his reasons for supporting it.

First, he said, it would have the effect of

> "Drawing more closely together, the bringing into terms of more familiar friendship, university students of all religious denominations. I wish, so far as in me lies, to extinguish all religious animosity, and to do everything that will tend to accomplish that, in my mind, most desirable object. Contrasting the relations at present existing between the Roman Catholic and Protestant denominations, I regret to be obliged to state, from my own personal experience, that they are not as cordial as they were some fifty years ago. In my view the most effectual remedy for this most deplorable state of things would be the solution I have suggested."

The Chief Baron's second reason had for its basis

> "The pride which, as a graduate of the University of Dublin, I take in that venerable institution. I join issue with those who suggest that the title of its prestige is confined to those of any particular religious denomination, or to those whose ideal of a University is that it must be a neutral as to religion."

Since he thought that the characteristic of a college ought to be such that it would be a place of religion as well as education, the title of all Irishmen to the University of

Dublin must exist, irrespective of the particular which, in the Trinity College of his day, was associated with education, research and learning.

Finally, said Palles, the dual college scheme would be a most effective stimulus to the preservation of high standards of university education in the country. He had been accused, he said, as a member of the Senate of the Royal University, of advocating the retention of high standards, and he retorted that he would not be willing to reduce them merely because some other institution offered equivalent degrees on easier terms. " I do not understand," he said, rather tartly, " the principle of a University or examining body endeavouring to compete in cheapness."

He added that the new college which he envisaged would have the advantage of affording an opportunity for closer contacts between ecclesiastical and lay students, and he felt that much benefit would result from the students of Maynooth College resorting there for their pre-theological studies. " There are few Roman Catholic gentlemen," said the Chief Baron, " who do not regret that their habits of thought and those of the Roman Catholic priesthood are not more closely coincident."

A great deal of his evidence to the Robertson Commission was taken up with the elaboration of this scheme for a new college in the University of Dublin. In particular, he considered the new college must possess a Faculty of Applied Science, and his views on this point are of considerable contemporary interest:

> " My view is that science, to be properly taught, must be brought up to the university. . . . I think that the university training is the capping of education in reference to every branch of education. For instance, in reference to Applied Science, my view is that a man with a University education will approach the question of Applied Science in a wholly different way from that in which the same subject will be approached by a man, although an able man, who has not had a university training; in other words, that there is something in a university training that will enable the mind to grasp, consider, and determine questions, in all sciences and in all subject-

matters of education, in a manner different from a mind not trained in a university. I would compare a university training to the sharpening of a knife. A knife so sharpened will perform a number of operations upon various subject-matters in a manner that never can be accomplished by a blunt knife. I consider that the sharp knife of the trained university man, when directed to Applied Science, will bring his knowledge to a point which cannot be reached by the untrained mind, although he may have a fair education in Applied Science."

All this involved the provision of adequate financial help by way of scholarships and grants for the student who could not afford to pay: "The child of the day labourer would be able, in time, to compete among those who ultimately seek to obtain the offices of Lord Chancellor and other high positions in the State." Women also entered into the Chief Baron's scheme, and he said that provision would have to be made for their residential halls.

It is a source of some satisfaction to the present writer that, in one respect, the Chief Baron's views have proved to be prophetic. One of the questions put to him was whether he thought the provision of a new university in Belfast was desirable. To this he replied:

"I wish here to remark, in concurrence with some of the previous witnesses, that, in my opinion, a University in Belfast would be a most useful institution, that it would not interfere with either Trinity College or the new university in Dublin, but would develop along entirely new lines. I have some acquaintance with the North of Ireland, in consequence of frequently going as judge of Assize on the North-eastern Circuit, during which we are often from two to three weeks in the city of Belfast. I think that you might have in Belfast a type of university new to Ireland, but of an admirable description. . . .

"The Belfast people, the people of the North of Ireland are eminently a practical people, and if the endowment of the Belfast College is increased, and if it is allowed to develop on its own lines . . . my idea is that, without saying anything as to what its ultimate success may be in classical learning, it will develop according to the lines which seem to be prevalent in Belfast—those lines which lead to remunerative employment, and that you will have a University there which will do more than anything else in the North of Ireland to repair some of our deplorable loss in higher education."

This, then, was the comprehensive scheme put forward by Palles for the final settlement of the Irish university question; and it was not through any fault of his that it was not the one ultimately adopted. In advocating it, he stated his views unequivocally:

> " My desire for the improvement of higher education, a matter that I have longed for all my life, does not depend upon any question of denomination or sect: I desire the same thing for all the subjects of the King. My view is for Ireland: I am anxious that all Irishmen shall be able to compete on equal terms with other citizens of the Empire, and to take their share in the government of the Empire."

Here we see the ultimate expression of an idea which had been germinating in the mind of the speaker over a period of many years. He recalled the long struggle of his fellow-Catholics for religious and civil equality, and now he saw that the last barrier to that equality, educational disparity at a university level, was about to fall. If it could be demolished, he considered, then a final solution to the Irish problem itself might be at hand. The fact that the events of the succeeding twenty years were to witness the fragmentation of the United Kingdom, does not disprove his theory; it merely shows that the remedy came too late.

As it happened, the report of the Robertson Commission proved ineffectual, as the exclusion of Trinity College from its terms of reference prevented any solution along the lines adumbrated by the Chief Baron. Lord Dunraven's later scheme was soon abandoned, but when the Liberals came to power in January, 1906, a new effort was made to arrive at a settlement.

In March, 1906, James Bryce, the Chief Secretary, decided to appoint another Commission, this time on Trinity College. With a view to placating Nationalist opinion, Bryce approached John Redmond and asked him

to name two suitable persons to serve on it. Redmond
nominated Douglas Hyde and Denis Coffey, and suggested
that the terms of reference should be strictly limited to
Trinity College. He added that " we could not regard the
Lord Chief Baron as a satisfactory appointment to represent our views on the Commission." This puzzled Bryce,
and he replied: " As to Chief Baron Palles, I don't know
him personally and I have no predilection, but so far have
not heard of any Catholic layman likely to carry equal
weight." A fortnight later, the Chief Secretary was to write
to Redmond that

> " As I have not heard from you the name of any other
> Irish Catholic of weight and reputation and academic
> experience equal to Palles, I have asked the latter to sit on
> the Trinity College Commission."

Redmond's biographer suggests that the proposal to
nominate Palles was distasteful to the Nationalist leader, in
view of the fact that he was thought to be opposed to
Home Rule in any form. On this point, the available
evidence is indecisive, but one thing is certain: he was
intensely Irish, in the sense that he approved of the principle that Irish affairs should be managed by Irishmen in
the interest of Ireland.

In the report of the Trinity College Commission, which
was published in 1907, Palles repeated his plan for two
colleges in the University of Dublin, though a majority of
the members wanted to include the Queen's Colleges as
well. Meanwhile, Bryce himself was formulating yet
another scheme. It was, in effect, a revision of the
Gladstone plan of 1873, and was accepted by the Catholic
bishops, by the Royal University, and by the Presbyterian
community. The Queen's College, Belfast, was not favourable, and Bryce's suggestions received their ultimate rejection at the hands of Trinity College, within which a
strenuous resistance was organised. That College was not
unanimous in its opposition, however, for in a statement
submitted to the Royal Commission, and signed by twelve
Junior Fellows and eight Professors, a series of safeguards

for Catholic students resorting to Trinity were proposed. A committee of Catholic laymen favoured a plan of integration, and there is no reason to believe that the opposition to it in the College itself could not have been overcome in the face of a really lasting settlement. The Catholic hierarchy, however, flatly refused to countenance it and said that " under no circumstances will the Catholics of Ireland accept a system of mixed education in Trinity College as a solution to their claim." In point of fact, the lay Catholics of Ireland were given no opportunity of expressing their views on the matter. The decisive moment in Irish university history had passed. The intransigence of the Trinity conservative group and of the Catholic hierarchy had between them destroyed for ever the possibility of a solution along lines which would have rendered the country's greatest educational foundation acceptable to all Irishmen.

It was left to Bryce's successor, Augustine Birrell, to work out the final settlement. Under his proposals there were to be two new universities; one a federal university at Dublin for Catholics, and embracing the Queen's Colleges of Cork and Galway, together with a new Dublin college, and Maynooth as a recognised institution; the other at Belfast, and erected out of the old Queen's College there. Both were to be free from religious tests and debarred from using their endowments for religious purposes.

Trinity College opinion was favourable to the Birrell scheme, for it did not affect the College. The Presbyterians expressed disapproval of it as a breach of the non-sectarian principle, but by the end of 1908 the National University of Ireland and the Queen's University of Belfast had been created by separate charters.

The legislation providing for these new arrangements was to come into force within two years after its enactment, and two bodies of Commissioners were set up, charged with the duty of drafting the statutes and appointing the staffs of the new universities. There was also a Joint Committee which was empowered to make schemes for the transfer to one or other of the foundations of the property of the former Royal University and the Queen's College, Belfast.

The chairman of the Dublin Commission was an obvious choice, and the appointment of Palles was soon announced, with Archbishop Walsh as a prominent member. For a man in his seventy-seventh year, the work was extremely onerous. There were visits to Liverpool, Manchester, Leeds and London, in order to take evidence on the matter of higher technological studies. There were frequent consultations in Dublin and Belfast, between members of the Joint Committee. The chairman of the Belfast Commission, Judge Shaw, was an old friend of the Chief Baron, and his sudden death in April, 1910, deprived the whole university movement of a wise counsellor. His successor, Sir Samuel Dill, was later to pay tribute to the work of Palles in these protracted negotiations. Writing to the Chief Baron on the latter's retirement from the Bench in 1916, he voiced his praise in no uncertain terms, a view that was fully shared by the Vice-Chancellor of the Queen's University, the Reverend Thomas Hamilton.

Much of the work involved the drudgery of draftsmanship, and in this Palles was assisted by two members of the Bar, D. F. Brown, K.C., and James A. Murnaghan, who afterwards graced the Supreme Court in the Irish Free State. Progress was commendably swift, however, and the new University College, Dublin, was open by the end of 1909.

Despite his loyalty to his own University and the fact that it took pride of place in his mind, it is not too much to say that Palles was the effective progenitor of the National University of Ireland. He was proud of his connection with Clongowes and with the Jesuits, and he had always taken a benevolent interest in their institution, the old University College in St. Stephen's Green, Dublin, which had carried on the work of Newman's Catholic University. In 1894, indeed, he had taken a prominent part in the foundation of a new sodality to care for the spiritual needs of the students of that College, and he had delivered the inaugural address to the new organisation. Now, when he perceived that there was no possibility of his own plan being put into effect, he was magnanimous enough to give his services in the establishment of the new federal University. Today, it is pleasant to recall, his name is perpetuated in the Dublin College, in the form of a noble collection of legal books, bought after his death by Archbishop Walsh, and presented to the College as his lasting memorial.

In presenting the Chief Baron for the Degree of Doctor in Laws, *honoris causa*, at the University of Cambridge in 1910, the Public Orator, after making graceful reference to the recipient's academic prowess and skill in mathematical learning, went on:

> ". . . Qui religioni suae devotissimus, in Hibernia tota omnium bonorum pacem et concordiam ante omnia exoptavit; qui propter insignem juris peritiam judicis summi ad dignitatem est evectus; qui de patriae Universitatibus, de populi sui Universitate nova, de toto denique populo melius educando, deliberationibus plurimis summa industria, summa prudentia, interfuit."

These are noble words, spoken of one who made a lasting contribution to Irish educational advancement, and it is to be hoped that those who came after him and who now enjoy the fruits of his labours, pause occasionally to spare a thought for the man whose "view was for Ireland."

XIV

THE LAST YEARS

THE disappearance of the Exchequer Division as a separate entity on the first day of 1898 marked the end of an era. For the Chief Baron, the change was of peculiar significance. He was now the sole survivor of an extinct system, and was left with nothing but his precedence and his memories of the times that were gone.

At the coming of the new century, he had become a judicial institution for, by 1904, he had completed thirty years upon the Bench. Of his contemporaries in 1874, there was but one survivor, Vice-Chancellor Chatterton, and he retired in that very year. New figures had appeared on the scene and, in truth, it can be said that the Irish courts were now adorned with more illustrious lawyers than at any time in their history.

The great seal was in the hands of Edward Gibson, Lord Ashbourne, who had first become Chancellor in 1885, who held that office again from 1886 to 1892 with the unprecedented honour of a seat in the Cabinet, and who had returned on the fall of the Liberals in 1895 to spend another decade as head of the Court of Appeal. With him sat Gerald FitzGibbon, a man who combined erudition with a pronounced feeling of justice, and Hugh Holmes, whose subtlety of thought was tempered with a sense of humour which makes his reported judgments a source of the greatest enjoyment. At this time, too, Ashbourne could call on the assistance of Samuel Walker, the Liberal ex-Lord Chancellor who was to return to office once again in 1905.

Of the judges who had sat with Palles in the Exchequer Division, the only survivor was William Drennan Andrews. Andrews was a precise man, possessed of a fund of accurate legal learning, whose mildness of judicial manner was equalled only by the severity of his sentences. Legal ability in the family appears to have been hereditary, for his nephew, Sir James Andrews, Bart., became the third Lord Chief Justice of Northern Ireland.

At the Bar, there were two men, from opposite ends of the country, who were to achieve the most exalted position in their profession. One, Redmond John Barry, from Cork, was cut off in his prime, having in his short but brilliant career achieved every legal prize open to him. A silk within eleven years of his call, Solicitor-General at thirty-nine, Barry was Lord Chancellor of Ireland at forty-five. Two years later, he died, mourned by all who knew him. It is pleasant to be able to record that his son, Sir Patrick Barry, now occupies an honoured place in the Queen's Bench Division in London.

The other, John Atkinson, a native of Belfast, was slightly younger than Palles, having been called in 1865. His services to the Conservatives as an Irish Law Officer were recognised by his belated elevation to the House of Lords in 1905. There he took part in the judicial business of the House until 1928, being endowed, as his biographer put it, with

> "an inflexible sense of duty which enabled him to steer undaunted a straight course through the stormy seas of Irish political life during a period when navigation was by no means easy, and to resist the strong pressure put upon him to resign . . . in order to satisfy the requirements of political party leaders."

It should be explained that through the years, the distribution of the court-rooms at the Four Courts building underwent a number of changes. The abolition of the Common Pleas Division made additional accommodation available to the Queen's Bench, and the room on the right of the entrance hall was assigned to the Chief Baron for the Exchequer Division. Here, contrary to the normal practice in Divisional Courts, Palles sat on the extreme right of the Bench, with Dowse (later Andrews) in the middle, and James Murphy on the left. After 1898, this room, now re-named "Queen's Bench No. 2," became the joint habitat of all the common law judges, but by tacit consent, the Chief Baron continued to occupy it as his own. When sitting at *nisi prius*, indeed, he would always empanel his own jury there.

Sitting in the Court of Appeal; constituting Divisional Courts to hear writs of *certiorari*; trying actions at *nisi prius*; and, above all, going circuit; these were the contributions of the Chief Baron in the last decade of his career on the Bench, and it is at this stage of his judicial life that he is now remembered by those few who survive to convey their impressions of his qualities. He was a hardworking judge, he took his duties seriously, and he gave the greatest satisfaction to litigants.

In particular, his delicacy of mind revolted from the ordeal of the capital trial, and the imposition of the judgment of death always caused him great anguish. Amongst his private papers there are to be found many draft letters in reply to various Lords-Lieutenant, taking his opinion as a trial judge on the exercise of the prerogative of clemency. In all these cases, he went into the most minute detail, examining every facet of the evidence, and if a petition for a reprieve went unanswered, it was surely not due to any failure on his part to place the arguments for and against the condemned prisoner before those whose duty it was to respite the penalty in a proper case.

Many anecdotes have been told—and re-told—of his character as a judge. Most of them illustrate those dominant features of his character, his simplicity and his modesty. On one occasion he tried, with a special jury, an action upon a promissory note. Adverting to the circumstances under which the instrument had been given, he told the jury : —

> " In order that you may understand the legal aspects of this case, it is necessary that I should explain to you as representing the merchant princes of this city the meaning and effect of a composition in bankruptcy."

The city was Cork: the foreman and two of the special jurors had recently carried such an arrangement with their creditors; and the discomfiture of the jurors in question was surpassed only by the delight of the audience.

His modesty was proverbial. At the county Kerry Assizes in Tralee, Peter O'Brien and Palles were the going judges. The High Sheriff called to know whether they would like to drive with their escort to Mass on the Sunday. " Peter," who was not averse to a little pomp, took the opinion of his brother. " Well, Peter," replied the Chief Baron, " you may make a fool of yourself if you like, but I'm going to walk!"

Maurice Healy relates a charming tale of the old man's humility when, as a very junior member of the Munster Bar, it was thought by some that the Chief Baron had suggested that Healy had acted dishonourably in presenting a case to the jury. The Chief was told by a senior member of the circuit. His reaction was characteristic of his greatness. At the sitting of the Court, he addressed Healy, saying: —

> " I have been told that this morning when addressing the jury I used words which might be understood as imputing dishonourable conduct to you in your conduct of the case. As dishonour is a word which I am sure I could never properly associate with your name, I have sent for you to express my regret with the same publicity as attached to my error."

Of those who practised before Palles, Mr. Justice W.E. Wylie recalls his first appearance at the county Tyrone Assizes, at Omagh, in 1905, when he received a dock brief to defend a prisoner charged with burglary, and he remembers with pleasure the help he received from the old man in the conduct of the case—culminating in a direction to the jury to acquit.

Shortly afterwards, he appeared before the Chief again, this time at Cavan. The case was a civil bill appeal, in an action for goods sold and delivered. Here, he says, he was hampered by the fact that his client, the plaintiff, had kept no books and so his proofs were of the flimsiest. As a result, the cross-examination of the defendant left much to be desired. Palles listened, the grim visage becoming grimmer, and all the signs of an impending eruption beginning to manifest themselves—the spasmodic kicking of the Bench, the rapid turning of the head, as if its owner was endeavouring to bite off his ear. At last, he barked, " See, see, young man, do you not know how to conduct a case against a *de*fendant for shop goods?" Counsel's reply, to the effect that he could not manufacture evidence, was stifled by the interjection, " Leave him to me!" The Chief fixed the unfortunate defendant with one of his most terrible glares, and said: "Now, sir, why do you not pay your lawful debts?" A stammering admission followed, and there was a decree for the full amount—with costs.

Perhaps, the most striking of all his characteristics was one which is lamentably lacking in many of his fellow-countrymen. Palles had what Saint James includes amongst the characteristics of wisdom—a readiness to receive impressions and to change his mind. The apostle may have thought it a characteristic of wisdom, but some Irishmen, it is to be feared, regard it as a mortal sin. He once told a friend that when he was appointed to the Exchequer, he kept before him a card on which was written, " Keep your mind open and your mouth shut. When you open your mouth you shut your mind." On the Bench, he never expressed an opinion, and so never became its advocate.

In a case which appears in the law reports, *Barrett v. Harold,* an action for assault was brought to vindicate a claim to be an *ex officio* Poor Law Guardian. The County Court judge dismissed the action, and Palles affirmed the decision on appeal, but stated a case. He sat with another judge in a Divisional Court to try the case stated and adhered to his former opinion. His brother judge dissented, and there was a re-argument before Palles and two others. Palles delivered the unanimous judgment of the Court, reversing himself.

On another occasion, he made an order adverse to a defendant's junior counsel, in his senior's absence. When the senior came into Court, he arrived to hear the Chief Baron discussing the form of the order to be made against

him. He protested against the proceedings, and pointed
out an error in a vital document before the Court. The
original was sent for, and the error rectified. Palles then
called on counsel for the plaintiff to deal with this new
point. "Twenty minutes ago," the latter protested, "the
Court expressed the opinion that I was entitled to carry
my motion."

> "Speaking for myself," said the Chief Baron, "I confess
> that I was foolish enough to make some observations to
> that effect, but you can learn a lot in twenty minutes, my
> young friend, if you will listen."

. . . . . .

There were other activities in these last years. We have
already seen that much of the Chief Baron's spare time
was devoted to the cause of university reform, and in, yet,
another educational field he played a notable part. This
was in connection with his old school, Clongowes.

At the turn of the century, Clongowes Wood College
occupied a commanding position in the educational life
of the country. Virtually all the Catholic landed gentry and
a large proportion of the Catholics of the professional
classes owed their early training to the academy in the
county Kildare and its contemporary prestige was immense.
Of its alumni, many occupied the most influential posts in
the country. John Naish had been Lord Chancellor ; Peter
O'Brien was Lord Chief Justice of Ireland; Sir Nicholas
O'Connor was Ambassador at the Court of St. Petersburg;
and it was only natural that Palles, himself a most distinguished son of the school, should take a lively interest
in its welfare.

A tangible result of this interest was the foundation of
the Clongowes Union, the inaugural meeting of which was
held on 29th June, 1897, at Number 28, Fitzwilliam Place.
The idea was that of the Chief Baron, who was most
anxious that the bonds of friendship formed at school
should be continued in after life. Later that year, the first
banquet of the Union was held at the Shelbourne Hotel,

at which Palles presided. In what was described at the time as " a rousing speech " he outlined the objects of the society, stressing the importance of the school in Irish life, and pointing out with pride that of the two Catholics who had held the office of Lord Chancellor since the Reformation, one was a Clongowes man.

His election as President of the Union was a foregone conclusion, and he occupied that position until he died. Year after year, he presided at meetings and attended at the school for the annual reunion. Perhaps the most pleasing photographs of the Chief Baron are those which caught him on these occasions—a little man standing, hat in hand, with a whimsical smile, often with Bessie by his side, always surrounded by the schoolboys for whom he must, indeed, have been an awe-inspiring figure. The culmination of his long tenure of office came in 1914, when Clongowes celebrated the centenary of its foundation. It was just seventy years since Palles had first gone there; and as he listened to the noble oratory of John Redmond on that day, one wonders what memories passed through his mind.

In the material sphere, too, he displayed a continuous solicitude for the school. At the annual meeting of the Union in 1905 he announced his intention of presenting a gold medal for mathematical competition amongst the pupils. Later, he confessed that the motive impelling him to make this gift was the fact that in his early days insufficient attention was paid to mathematics at Clongowes, because, he thought, the Trinity Fellowships (which placed great weight on mathematical ability) were then closed to Catholics, and so there was nothing to be gained in encouraging the study at the school.

The Palles Medal became an institution at Clongowes. Until his death, the Chief Baron presented it annually, a custom which was continued by his niece so long as she lived. After her death, she directed her executors to invest a sum of money for its perpetuation, and, today, it is still regarded as the premier award.

The other object of his munificence to the school, the

altar in the boys' chapel, is also characteristic of his innate
modesty, the only indication of the identity of the donor
being a statue of St. Christopher on the reredos. One
wonders whether many of those who are now alumni of
the school know the origin of this handsome gift.

. . . .

The passage of the years saw the disappearance of many
of the Chief's old friends, but mingled with the sadness of
their loss there was always the excitement of making new
acquaintances. He never grew old, in the sense of a man
who cuts himself off from contemporary life. In 1911,
when he was eighty, he was invited by the Queen's University of Belfast to unveil a memorial tablet to his friend,
Judge Shaw.

In acceding to the invitation, he excelled himself, and
there can be few more eloquent testimonies to a man who
did honour to his profession, his University and his
country. One phrase in the address on Shaw strikes a major
chord, for it might have been spoken of Palles himself:

"He was well stored, when I met him, with settled and
fixed convictions upon a number of subjects, social,
economic and political, quite unusual in a man of his age;
and from those convictions it was practically impossible
to move him. But if he had, and abided by, his convictions, and was not slow to give expression to them at the
proper time; so, too, did he allow to others the right of
having and expressing their views. I found in him a
remarkable tolerance of the convictions of those who
differed from him, and that he was always willing and
anxious to analyse and discuss conflicting views, so as to
withdraw as many questions as possible from the field of
difference, and arrive, as a basis of action, at so much of
the divergent opinions as might be common to all."

The speaker might have been drawing a portrait of his
own character and it is not too much to surmise that the
close bond between Palles and Shaw sprang from this
temperamental similarity—tolerance.

In 1913, the Queen's University recognised Palles's contribution to law and education by conferring upon him the honorary degree of LL.D. The expiring Royal University had bestowed a similar honour in 1909, and reference has already been made to the action of Cambridge in this matter in 1910. The last honour came to him in the summer of 1914, when his own University transmuted the LL.D. of 1860 to an honorary one.

A belated friend and a regular correspondent in this period was the Chief Secretary, Augustine Birrell. They had first met at the time of the university negotiations. As time passed, however, Palles became more and more alarmed by the Government's apparent inability to prevent the growth of disaffection in Ireland, north and south. The repeal of the Arms Act in 1906 had seemed to him to be a piece of sheer folly, and the fact that the prohibition on the importation of arms was not reimposed until 1913 (in circumstances of doubtful validity) was strongly condemned by him. The validity of the ban was being tested in the Courts by the Ulster Unionists, and a suggestion by the Law Officers to the effect that these proceedings could be compromised by withdrawing the ban, was regarded by Palles as running contrary to all accepted notions of peace preservation.

There were other and less serious issues with Birrell. On one occasion the Chief Secretary wrote to the Chief Baron in considerable perturbation, asking him whether he had ever decided that the Franciscans were an illegal organisation in Ireland. Birrell was being assailed by an Irish member in the Commons, who had alleged that the members of this worthy community in Athlone were having their premises rated because they were illegal! Palles was able to reassure his correspondent on this point which, one feels, may well have been taken in the first place with the object of discomfiting the Irish administration.

During his last five years on the Bench the Chief Baron's work went on at full pressure. In the spring of 1911, he was on the Munster Circuit with Dodd; in the summer, he travelled the North-West with Holmes. In 1912, his companions were John Gibson on the Leinster, and Dodd on the North-East. Next year, he delivered the gaols of the North-West and the North-East, again with Holmes and Dodd in the commission. In that year, he received the honour of being summoned to London to sit on the Judicial Committee of the Privy Council, in an appeal from Canada which involved complicated questions of marriage law.

Those who took part in the case realised that the almost mythical reputation of Palles was well-founded. The hearing occupied the best part of a week and, until the final day, the Chief Baron maintained an unwonted silence. As counsel for the respondents was about to sit down, however, he suddenly interjected: "What authority have you for that proposition?" "My Lord," said counsel, "I have the best possible authority, an opinion of this honourable Committee." "If you tell me this Committee has so decided," replied Palles, jerking his head from side to side in characteristic fashion, "I am reluctant to depart from their view, but, in my opinion, they were wrong." Thenceforward, the old man assumed complete control of the proceedings, and largely influenced the findings reached by the Board.

That evening, according to legend, the Chief Baron dined with Frank Kennedy at their London hotel and afterwards they went to a theatre. When they returned, they were about to part for the night when Palles observed: "Goodnight, my dear Frank, I have not enjoyed myself so much for years," and then, after a little hesitation, "But, see, see, in my opinion, I am drunk.'"

Not content with this performance, moreover, he crossed straight from Liverpool to Belfast, and commenced the business of trying special jury cases at the Summer Assizes, a remarkable achievement for a man almost eighty-one years old.

Time was passing. The onset of the world war did little to upset the even tenor of his ways. As it happened, however, 1915 was to be his last year on circuit, and it was fitting that he should have chosen the Leinster, in which his old circuit, the Home, had been merged. He sat for the last time in a Home Circuit town, Naas, on Thursday, 15th July, 1915, almost exactly sixty-three years after he had first gone there as a raw junior.

We are fortunate in possessing a detailed account of one of the cases which he tried on that last circuit, at Wexford. One or two minor aspects of the cause have found their way into the law reports, under the name of *Gethings v. Cloney*, but these bald statements scarcely do justice to a proceeding which seems to have produced enormous excitement in the county Wexford. It was fitting that such a case should come before the Chief Baron on his last assize; and he appears to have enjoyed it thoroughly.

Gethings and Cloney were what would be described in Ireland as " strong " farmers. For a number of years prior to 1915 there had been friction between them, the *casus belli* being a stream which flowed from Cloney's land to that of Gethings, who constantly complained that his neighbour's cattle polluted it in every conceivable manner. The dispute was at one stage settled between the parties by a formal agreement between them by which Cloney had agreed to fence certain places against his own cattle. This was found to be impracticable, and Cloney, therefore, issued a writ against Gethings. When the action first came on for hearing, counsel concocted another agreement, and the going judge of assize was asked to strike the case out on the ground that the parties were about to settle it. Cloney had second thoughts, refused to execute the settlement and adopted the novel course of suing his own solicitor for negligence. He failed in this action, and so a year or two later the case was set down again, this time before the Chief Baron.

Leading counsel for the plaintiff was D. J. O'Brien, K.C. O'Brien was an able but rather timid man, who was known on the Leinster Circuit as " Anxious Dan," a title which he had acquired in a ribald ballad composed for performance at Bar dinners. He led Tom Bodkin, who has since achieved

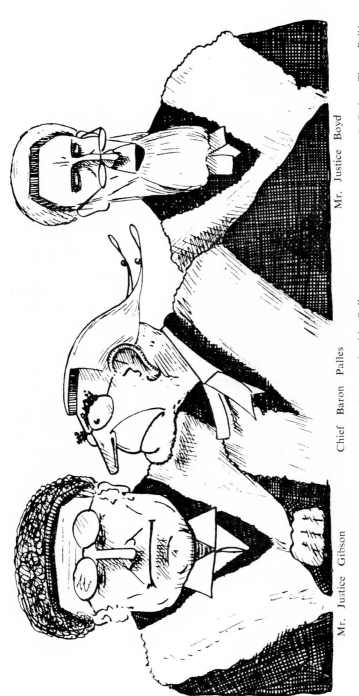

Mr. Justice Gibson   Chief Baron Palles   Mr. Justice Boyd

The C. B. consults his Colleagues.

By Professor Thomas Bodkin.

fame in the world of artistic criticism. The defendant mustered William K. Gibson, K.C.; Annesley St. George De Renzy, K.C., and Cecil fforde—a formidable battery of talent, all renowned for their sardonic wit.

Dan O'Brien, in common with the other members of the Bar, had a wholesome respect for the Chief Baron, though, like all of them, he liked and admired him. He did not, however, relish going into Court before Palles with a case in which the merits were disputable and in which he would be opposed by such formidable metal. As a result, he suggested to his instructing solicitors, who were known locally as " The Corsican Brothers," that the case was eminently one for settlement.

At the consultation, held on the eve of the trial, the settlement was urged on Cloney. It was a suggestion which he did not receive with any favour. In the end, as a matter of routine civility, Bodkin was asked for his views, and he strongly advised against any such course, pointing out that the plaintiff was suing for damages for breach of an agreement that had been duly executed between the parties, and that the Chief Baron, though he would scarcely award heavy damages, would certainly, because of the legal strength of their position, give a verdict which would carry costs. It was decided, therefore, that battle should be joined on the morrow.

Next morning, the Chief Baron sat in a crowded Court. Dan O'Brien had hardly begun to state the plaintiff's case when, from the opposite side, there arose a chorus of interruptions referring to the settlement which counsel had drafted a couple of years before and from which Cloney had backed out. After a while Palles remarked, " See, see, Mr. O'Brien, I'd like to look at this settlement." Dan, a trifle obsequiously, replied: " Of course, anything your Lordship wishes to see we will be only too pleased to show." As the draft deed had somewhat exposed the weakness of the case, there was a hurried whisper from Bodkin: " He has no right to see it; it is not pleaded; it has nothing to do with our case." At that Dan rather lost his head and, turning to the Chief Baron, exclaimed, "My Lord, my junior does not think you ought to see it."

The Chief Baron shook with amusement, and replied, "Mr. O'Brien, do nothing which you think your junior would not approve of." Gibson and his colleagues made the most of this incident; and from thence on almost every question asked or statement made by the unfortunate "Anxious Dan" was greeted by a surreptitious "Does your junior know you're out?," or "Have you got your junior's leave to ask that?"

The hearing lasted for the best part of two days, and some of the evidence was extremely amusing. One of the plaintiff's sons was an amateur photographer who had spent a great deal of time watching his neighbour's cattle and succeeded in producing some striking prints, showing them behaving very badly indeed; these greatly impressed the Chief Baron. When the evidence closed, however, Dan O'Brien had his revenge on his junior counsel. He turned to him and said: "Tom, you will now address the Court."

Professor Bodkin, who has since confessed to the present writer that "my practice was not big enough to put any great strain on me" and who, in consequence, had had plenty of time to make up his brief, spoke for about an hour. During the first twenty minutes Palles did not utter, but followed closely what he had to say, nodding occasionally in assent or shaking his head. During the next twenty minutes he intervened with a good many questions and comments, all of them relevant and helpful. By now, it will be appreciated that the Chief Baron was not a silent judge. He participated fully in every case that came before him, but never closed his mind until the last word had been said by counsel and witnesses. As one member of the Bar, who practised before him, put it,

> "He gave the impression of enjoying his work intensely, seeking dispassionately to bring each particular case to a right conclusion, and ready to collaborate with anyone concerned who could help to that end."

When junior counsel for Cloney sat down, the Chief slapped his desk emphatically, kicked the front of the

Bench (the normal symptoms of a mild excitement), leant over and tapped the wig of Frank Kennedy, who sat below him. As Frank Kennedy rose and turned to him, he exclaimed in ringing tones, almost petulantly, " See, see, Frank, you were entirely wrong. He made an excellent speech." There was a ripple of laughter through the Court, and the Chief shared the amusement. Everyone realised what had happened. Frank Kennedy, a kindly man, had warned him that Bodkin was an inexperienced tyro who might easily be put off by too frequent judicial interruptions and Palles, having curbed himself during the first part of the address, felt a little aggrieved. He promptly gave a decree, awarding £150 damages.

For the Chief Baron, life on circuit was a joyous affair. He loved circuit dinners, particularly in the company of the younger members, whom he always addressed by their surnames, though in Court he was particular to use, with characteristic emphasis, the prefix " Mister ". Of them, he once said: " I love to hear a young man make a good point; I feel I want to go down from the Bench and shake him by the hand."

The young men's admiration of their Chief Baron stopped just short of worship. He was interested in every topic that was raised in conversation. Professor Bodkin remembers him, one evening after dinner, punting himself across the floor in his chair towards a little group engaged in a discussion about the various breeds of dogs, exclaiming as he went: " See, see, Kinahan, what is that you're saying about the relative qualities of bull-dogs and bull-terriers?" Bob Kinahan was a lively junior for whom the Chief Baron had a considerable admiration. His diction in Court on the morning after a special dinner in the Bar mess was apt to be a little pedantic. On one such occasion he said to a country man in the witness box: " Having regard to the *locus in quo,* demonstrate to his Lordship the point of impact." The Chief Baron blandly remarked: " Ah, see, see, Mr. Kinahan, just ask him where he was hit."

On Christmas Day, 1915, the Chief Baron celebrated

his eighty-fourth birthday, and for some weeks during the preceding term he had been indisposed, having, it seems, suffered a slight stroke. In the New Year, he was unable to attend the Benchers' meeting on the first day of term, though he expressed the hope that he would be well again in a few weeks. He did manage to sit again before that momentous Easter, though the dire events of April and their aftermath disrupted the business of the Courts.

As the spring progressed, the distressing symptoms which had appeared did not abate. Palles, with his high sense of duty, was most unwilling to continue to serve on the Bench if his faculties were in any danger of a sudden impairment. He must have recalled the criticisms that had been levelled against Lefroy and Blackburne at an earlier time, and resolved that he would lay down his charge just as soon as it became apparent to him that he could no longer perform it. The best medical advice at his disposal inclined towards the view that a continuance in office might spell disaster. The Chief Baron did not hesitate. On 7th June, 1916, he wrote to the Prime Minister, offering his resignation from the Bench. Four days later Asquith replied :

My Lord,
  I have the honour to acknowledge your Lordship's letter of the 7th in which you tender your resignation of the office of Lord Chief Baron.
  I received your Lordship's proposal with extreme regret, knowing well the inestimable value of the service which you have rendered in one of the highest posts on the Irish Bench for the best part of half a century. As an old practitioner, I venture to say that the judgments of Palles, C.B., are held in as high esteem by English and American as by Irish lawyers.
  I cannot, however, in view of what you report as to the state of your health, ask you to reconsider your decision, but I beg you to accept the assurance of my sympathy and respect.
                    Your Lordship's faithful servant,
                                    H. H. Asquith.

Though the resignation was not to become effective until 5th July, 1916, the news soon spread amongst his friends and colleagues and they hastened to join in expressions of regret. Barton wrote :

> " You were the sun in our firmament. But, if our sun has set, it leaves an afterglow which will never disappear; because there will remain with us the example, the memory and the tradition of the greatest judge that ever sat on our Bench."

Archbishop Walsh added his tribute, saying that he would be an irreparable loss to the Courts,

> " for which you have done so much to win for the administration of the law in this country the respect of all those whose respect is worth having."

Perhaps the most touching letter came from H.V. Yeo, the veteran Master of the King's Bench Division, when he said that he was

> " proud to remember I served for so many years under our ' Grand Old Man,' and, let me observe also, that I well remember him when he was our ' Grand Young Man ' . . . . . ."

A little time still remained. Palles had heeded his physician's warning and he had retired with his faculties unimpaired. Age had not dimmed his memory and those who knew him in retirement rejoiced to find him still retaining the quickness of discernment and the broad grasp of affairs which was pre-eminently his. Sir John Ross, who had come to live near Mountanville, became his weekly visitor and they spent much time discussing together the cases which came before the Court of Appeal or the House of Lords. Ross recalled one incident, which was typical of the man. Palles had a gold pencil which had been the terror of the Bar. When counsel stated a proposition of law, out came the pencil and with it he wrote down the name of some case on a slip, which he handed to his crier, Donovan, who would shortly return with the volume, whereby counsel was to be demolished. As the end approached, he asked his niece for the pencil. She brought it to him and he gave it to her with an injunction that when he had gone it was to be delivered to his friend, John Ross.

In these days of seclusion he continued to be a most versatile talker. While he freely uttered criticisms of men and ideas, he was never harsh or unjust. His profound insight into character was matched only by his almost childlike simplicity. Even at this advanced age there was manifest to the observer an atmosphere of intense mental energy. His long life at the Bar and on the Bench had equipped him with a fund of anecdote, and he was a capital raconteur. As always, he loved the companionship of the younger men and he mourned the passing of so many of them in the Great War. With one, at least, an old Clongownian, Ambrose Davoren, he had been wont to discuss legal topics as with an equal.

The last few months of his life were darkened by the knowledge that Ireland was in the grip of lawlessness and civil strife. The final usurpation of function of the King's Courts and the resulting collapse of the administration of justice were matters which were hidden from him—mercifully so, for he would have expressed his heartfelt detestation of them. His lifelong devotion to the principles of Liberalism was allied with a sincere belief in the Union as the true solution of Ireland's difficulties, and he viewed the activities of Gladstone and his successors in the leadership of the Liberal Party after 1886 as being conditioned by the aberration of Home Rule.

Now, however, the end of all earthly things was at hand, and though he passed his eighty-eighth birthday, only a few short weeks remained. With the New Year his strength ebbed rapidly and the final scene came on 14th February, 1920, very quietly, in the darkness of a winter's morning.

The sense of loss which possessed not only the legal profession but the whole of responsible opinion in Ireland was everywhere to be seen. A crowded meeting of Bench and Bar in the Court of Appeal heard the moving panegyrics pronounced by Sir James Campbell and Serjeant

Sullivan, and the newspapers at home and abroad vied with
one another to treat of his career in notices of unprecedented eulogy.

Christopher Palles rests in Glasnevin cemetery, in
Dublin, a short mile from the place of his birth and close
to his wife and to the devoted Bessie. Forty years have
passed since his death and his true memorial is to be
found in his life's work in the law. He did not believe that
the common law was perfect by nature, but rather that it
was constantly being perfected by art, by the cumulative
experience of succeeding generations, and that he was but
a humble instrument in this process. As his master, Coke
expressed it:

> "For reason is the life of law, nay the common law
> itself is nothing else but reason; which is to be understood
> of an artificial perfection of reason, gotten by long study,
> observation, and experience, and not of every man's
> natural reason; for *Nemo nascitur artifex.*"

Palles spent his whole life wondering what people could
see in him that was in any way better than appeared in
other men: such, one thinks, is the characteristic of giants.

XV

THE LEGACY OF CHRISTOPHER PALLES:

A POSTSCRIPT

THE story of a long and honourable judicial career had
drawn to a close. The name of Palles had become a byword
for all that is great and good in our legal system. When
he died human memory hardly penetrated to the time
when he was not upon the Irish Bench, and now that he
had departed from the scene his judgments, which in his
lifetime had been regarded with weighty respect, came to
be looked on with an almost religious awe. At a time so
closely removed from the event, critical analysis was
impossible, if not irreverent; and the passage of forty years
from his death has not eased the task.

For those unversed in the ways of the common law, the
work of a judge can scarcely evoke enthusiasm: but as
Mr. Justice Samuels has observed, " Palles lived in the
law and his decisions are his best memorial." It is in the
pages of the law reports from 1874 to 1916 that one must
seek the intellectual characteristics of the man, and it is in
the very profusion of his judicial utterances that one finds
difficulty in assessing their value. Today, perhaps, a more
objective approach is possible; the fact that a principle is
said to have been laid down by the Chief Baron will, in
the words of Lord Buckmaster in the House of Lords, give
recognition to " his great legal position," and " entitles all
his utterances to be regarded with attention;" it does not
always ensure, even in Ireland, that it will not be open to
unfavourable comment. One of the characteristic features
of our law, indeed—its inductive method of applying precedents—lends itself to a practice of discarding that which
is unwelcome and adopting that which suits the case in
hand.

If one is to appreciate the significance of the impact of Palles on the common law, it is necessary to appreciate that the separate history of that law in Ireland is a comparatively short one. The system was, it is true, introduced into the country in medieval times, but there is no reason to believe that it diverged in any notable respect from the parent root until the beginning of the last century—indeed, about the time of Palles's birth. The fact that Englishmen tended to occupy the places on the Bench; the fact that until 1849 there was virtually no indigenous system of legal education; and, above all, the fact that there were no printed reports of the Irish decisions upon which could be founded a native system of precedent, all contributed to this result. It is said of Lord Manners, who held the great seal in the 1820s, that he once addressed counsel thus: " Are you sure, Mr. Plunket, that what you have stated is the law?" " It unquestionably was the law half an hour ago," replied the advocate pulling out his watch ; " but by this time the packet boat has probably arrived, and I shall not be positive."

Regular series of Irish law reports did not appear much before 1827 ; and so the common law had but little more than fifty years to develop along its own lines before the Judicature Act replaced the old system of separate courts with a unified pattern. Palles, it can be said, advanced in his legal career surrounded by an increasing profusion of reported Irish law, and as a young barrister he saw that law coalesce into a distinct pattern of its own. Most of the members of the judiciary were now Irishmen, imbued with the local vagaries of the courts. By the time he had arrived at the head of the profession, Irish law had acquired most of those distinctive characteristics which it retains to this day. The existence of the House of Lords as a court of final appeal had not, as might have been expected, a unifying influence over the legal systems of the two islands. Proposals for an interchangeable Bench and Bar, much canvassed by Lord Brougham in the 1840s, came to nothing, and the presence in the Lords after 1868 of at least one Irishman ensured that full weight would be given to the existing differences.

While an accident of history placed Palles on the Irish Bench at a time when the common law had developed to its full maturity there, similar fortuitous circumstances ordained that when ultimately he came to take his seat in the Court of Appeal he should have for his judicial colleagues two or three individuals who were also to make important contributions to the law's elaboration. If an Irish lawyer were asked to suggest a particular period of time at which the country possessed a "strong" Court of Appeal, he would doubtless think of the twenty-five years preceding 1916. Porter, Barry, Holmes, FitzGibbon, Walker, Naish, and the two Gibsons—these were all Palles's judicial contemporaries and were eminently fitted to fill that exacting position.

Reading the law reports in the period, one is impressed by the marked difference in judicial approach of the various members of the Court. FitzGibbon and Lord Ashbourne, one feels, were pragmatists. They perceived the essential justice (or otherwise) of a litigant's cause, and they proceeded to cast about them for legal principles to justify a finding in his favour. Very different was the attitude of Holmes and Palles. For them, the essential efficacy of the common law, coupled with an awesome reverence for precedent, was the guiding spirit in its application. They enunciated principles, it is true, but both of them shunned needless generalisations or purely *à priori* expressions of view. For Palles, in particular, enunciation of principle was invariably guarded in the limitation of its application. A voluminous—sometimes, one fears, a laborious— examination of the authorities led to the inexorable conclusion.

Occasionally, indeed, his insistence on the strictest compliance with technical legal forms had unfortunate results. Thus in the leading case of *Pearson v. Dublin Corporation* (*1*), an action for breach of contract based on a fraudulent representation by the defendants' engineer, Palles non-

[1] [1907] 2 I.R. 27, 82, 537 ; [1907] A.C. 351.

suited the plaintiffs at the close of their case on the ground
that their claim could not be supported in the absence of
a certificate from the engineer. This ruling was reversed by
the King's Bench Division, before Lord O'Brien, C.J., and
Gibson, Boyd and Wright, J.J. The Court of Appeal, consisting of Lord Chancellor Walker, FitzGibbon and Holmes,
L.JJ., restored the Chief Baron's finding, and the House of
Lords, composed of Lord Chancellor Loreburn, and Lords
Halsbury, Macnaghten, James, Robertson, Atkinson and
Collins, reversed the Irish Court of Appeal and ordered a
new trial. The case was ultimately settled, but not before it
had been adjudicated on by no less than sixteen judges, and
not before the Chief Baron, taking a strong line on a technicality, had involved the parties in heavy costs.

With such a mass of material available, it would be easy
to devote a disproportionate amount of space to analysis of
his legal method and style. This is not practicable, however, and the most that can be done is to indicate here and
there some instances of his incisive application of the law-
making function of a judge.

Perhaps the branch of jurisprudence in which Palles
made his most lasting contribution was what is generally
called the law of torts, or civil wrongs. To speak of the law
of torts as the " law of wrongs ", indeed is probably a mis-
nomer; it might be more appropriate to speak of the law
for the creation and protection of rights. Its essential function has always been to delimit new grounds for the protection of human interests. It is not confined, like property
law, to developing rules for the transfer of things from one
person to another, nor as are the rules of the law of contracts, to the control of business relations. Constitutional law
exists to protect the citizen against legislation which im-
pairs fundamental interests, but the law of torts gives protection against harmful conduct in the entire range of
human interests.

A tort, moreover, may be a wrong only in the sense that the courts may require a defendant to pay for the harm which he has done by his entirely faultless activity. Thus the builder of a reservoir may be constructing something which is of benefit to the community, yet he will be made liable for the escape of water from it. Again, a manufacturer may be responsible for the harm to others done by the wrongful acts of his servants, or for harm caused to those servants in carrying out his business. Innocent trespass and the speaking or writing of innocent words which turn out to be defamatory, are additional illustrations of the principle that to say that such acts are " wrongful " is to misdescribe them. They are " tortious ", but only because in the conflict of interests the courts have concluded that justice is best served by placing the loss on the trespasser, the speaker, or the writer. The same is true of negligence, where the actor is doing as well as one of his limited skill can be expected to do. Tort, indeed, is a body of rules which provide compensation for harm caused by another, and the question whether or not the defendant's conduct is wrongful is of secondary importance.

There is another characteristic of the law of torts which made it a pliable instrument in the hands of the Chief Baron. It is dynamic ; it grows and expands to meet changing economic and social conditions. It was at this point that Palles was most free from the constraint of precedent ; for it was here that the common law judges, beginning with the simple notion of affording protection against physical interference with persons and things, created a vast system of rules by which virtually all human interests are now given protection.

All these features of the law appear when consideration is given to that most difficult concept known as negligence. The idea that one who causes harm to another is liable to answer for harm caused through his fault arose at a fairly early stage in the common law, but it was not until the industrial revolution of the nineteenth century, when the advent of machines made accidents common, that the idea became in any way refined. In its legal sense, " negligence "

includes all situations in which the defendant creates a like-
lihood of harm either physical or otherwise for which the
law will give redress if harm is suffered. It is not a state of
mind except in so far as it indicates an intent to cause
harm. Moreover, it is not a failure to do something; it is the
doing of something carelessly. Where a motor car injures
a pedestrian because of its failure to stop, caused by defective brakes, it is not the failure to repair the brakes
which is negligent; it is the driving with defective brakes.

One of the first cases heard by the Chief Baron after his
appointment was *Slattery v. Dublin, Wicklow and
Wexford Railway Co.* (2), which he tried at Wicklow
Spring Assizes with a jury in 1874. It was an action by a
widow to recover damages for the death of her husband.
The deceased had gone with some friends to the Lansdowne
Road railway station, near Dublin, to see an intending passenger off on the train. He crossed the rails by a level-
crossing, to the rear of a train standing in the station ; his
friends, from where they stood, could see an express train
approaching from the opposite direction, but Slattery could
not see it, and, on recrossing the line, he was killed by the
express. The driver of the express admitted that it was his
duty to blow his whistle at this point, and evidence was
tendered that he had done so. The deceased's friends said
that they did not hear it. The case was twice tried, and at
each trial there was a verdict for the plaintiff. The verdict
in the first trial, before FitzGerald B., was set aside upon
the ground of admission of illegal evidence. The second
trial was before Palles.

At the close of the plaintiff's case, counsel for the defendants asked the Chief Baron to withdraw it from the
jury, on the ground that there was no evidence of negligence on their part. Palles declined to do so, and in his
charge to the jury, he told them that if the driver had
whistled they should find for the defendant, but if he had
not, then they should consider whether there was want of
due care ; and he left it to them to say whether there was
contributory negligence on the part of Slattery.

²I.R. 8 C.L. 531 ; I.R. 10 C.L. 256 ; 3 App. Cas. 1155.

The jury at this second trial found for the plaintiff, and a motion was brought to set aside the verdict or, in the alternative, for a new trial. The Court of Common Pleas held that there was evidence of negligence proper to be submitted to the jury, that the Chief Baron's direction was correct in law, and that the question of contributory negligence had been properly left to them. An appeal was taken to the Court of Exchequer Chamber, in which Palles himself took part in the decision. Here the Court was equally divided, FitzGerald B., Dowse B., and Palles C. B., affirming the decision, while Whiteside C. J., Deasy B. and Barry J. thought that a verdict should be entered for the railway company, because of the contributory negligence of Slattery.

A further appeal was taken to the House of Lords, and the case was twice argued there before an opinion of the House was given. The majority upheld the decision of the Common Pleas (which had stood because of the equal division of opinion in the Exchequer Chamber), though Lords Hatherley, Coleridge and Blackburn dissented, on the ground that there had been enough evidence to show that Slattery was guilty of contributory negligence, and so might be non-suited. Thus the Chief Baron's direction to the jury was vindicated, though by a narrow majority.

Ten years later he had to consider the nature of the contributory negligence which would enable a trial judge to withdraw a plaintiff's case from a jury. In that case, *Coyle v. Great Northern Railway of Ireland* (3) he said

" That, to justify the judge in leaving the case to the jury, notwithstanding the voluntary act of the injured person which contributed to the injury complained of, the circumstances must be such as either, firstly, to make the question whether that act is negligent (either *per se,* or having regard to the conduct of the defendants inducing or affecting it), a question of fact; or, secondly, the circumstances must be such as to render reasonable an inference of fact, that the defendants, by using due care, could have obviated the consequences of the plaintiff's

³20 L.R. Ir. 409.

negligence. If the case be so clear that the determination of these two questions involves no inference of fact, it is for the judge and not for the jury."

This principle, which has been acted on in countless cases since it was first enunciated, was accepted by Dowse B., who sat with Palles, and he observed that

> "This case affords an apt illustration of the truth contained in the Laureate's lines, when he speaks of :—
>
> ' The lawless science of our law—
> That codeless myriad of precedent
> That wilderness of single instances.'
>
> "Here we have judges differing from one another, and, what is worse and more confusing, sometimes differing from themselves. Our duty is to endeavour to extract a principle from these ' single instances ', and this duty has been discharged by the Chief Baron in this case."

In 1890, legal proceedings which arose out of the disastrous Armagh railway accident led to the Chief Baron making a further important contribution to the law, when he held, in *Bell v. Great Northern Railway of Ireland* (4), that damages were recoverable for nervous shock suffered in consequences of a defendant's negligence, in the absence of any actual physical injury. The Privy Council, in an Australian appeal, had earlier decided to the contrary, but, said the Chief Baron,

> "The judgment assumes, as a matter of law, that nervous shock is something which affects merely the mental functions, and is not in itself a peculiar physical state of the body. This error pervades the entire judgment."

Here again, this was the starting point of a chain of judicial decisions in England, in Scotland, and in the United States (though the doctrine was received with reserve in the latter country), in which it has been held that

⁴26 L.R. Ir. 428.

in a proper case, the mere fact that the injury suffered is not physical will not prevent damages being awarded to the plaintiff.

The law with regard to the duties owed by the occupiers of premises to those who come on them with leave and licence, whether they be infants or adults, was laid down by the Chief Baron in the King's Bench Division in 1906, in the great case of *Cooke v. Midland Great Western Railway of Ireland* (5). There, the plaintiff was a child of between four and five years of age who was injured while playing on a turntable on the defendant's railway premises. Palles found for the plaintiff, not on the ground that there was any duty owed to child trespassers (as had been held in some of the American decisions), but because the habitual acquiescence of the railway company was sufficient evidence of the fact that the child was on the premises with the company's leave and licence. Palles was reversed by the Court of Appeal, but his judgment was restored by the unanimous opinion of the House of Lords. The case came in for a good deal of hostile criticism at a later date, the author of one of the standard legal textbooks describing the infant plaintiff as one of " a rabble of Irish raga-muffin raiders," a description which impelled another writer to plead that he was " the quite presentable son of a respectable chemist."

All these cases re-stated the broad principle of the scope of the duty of care owed by defendants not to infringe the interests of plaintiffs. The law of torts exists to protect against harmful conduct throughout the whole range of such human interests ; and nowhere is this more obvious than in those cases where the interest infringed is that of freedom of trade. Thus it was that a business dispute in the town of Lisburn gave rise to legal consequences of the most far-reaching dimensions and did much to influence future decisions.

In this case—*Quinn v. Leathem* (6)—Leathem was a

⁵[1908] 2 I.R. 242, 270 ; [1909] A.C. 229.
⁶[1899] 2 I.R. 667, 744 ; [1901] A.C. 495.

Lisburn butcher who employed non-union workmen. The defendants, who were members of the Belfast Butchers' Union, sought to enforce a " closed shop " in the trade, and asked Leathem to dismiss the non-union men. In addition, the Union refused to admit to membership Leathem's men, until he had first employed men already union members. As a result of these dealings, the defendants induced Leathem's employees to leave him and, in addition, they persuaded one of his customers in Belfast to cease to deal with him.

Leathem suffered considerable damage in his business, and he sued the defendants, the action coming on for hearing before Lord Justice FitzGibbon and a jury at Belfast Summer Assizes of 1896. By a coincidence, the senior judge of assize at Belfast on that occasion was the Chief Baron himself. The jury found for the plaintiff and returned a verdict for £200 damages, and the defendants moved for a new trial in the Queen's Bench Division, before O'Brien L.C.J., Palles C.B., Andrews and O'Brien JJ.

Writing more than sixty years after the event, it is not possible even now to say with certainty the extent to which the law will go to protect an interest of this type, and in 1898 the position was even more obscure. At that time, two decisions of the House of Lords reflected the current view, that it formed no part of the function of the courts to interfere with the free play of economic forces. In the words of Lord Halsbury, " All are free to trade upon what terms they like."

In the *Mogul Steamship Company Case* (7), the plaintiff alleged that the defendants, who were an assorted body of traders in China tea, had caused loss to him, a rival trader, by compelling certain merchants in China to cease to act as his agents, by means of a threat that if they continued to do so, the agency of the defendant's association would be withdrawn from them. There, it was held that there was no cause of action, since the defendants were merely taking

[7][1892] A.C. 25.

a justifiable measure of self-protection, and had acted with the lawful object of extending their trade.

A few years later, in *Allen v. Flood* (8), the House held that where a defendant, who was a delegate of an iron-workers' trade union, warned the plaintiff's employers that unless they discharged him, they would call a strike, and they had so discharged him, no action lay against the defendant. There had been no combination, and therefore although the defendant had acted maliciously, an improper motive would not give rise to a cause of action if no legal right had been infringed.

When the Lisburn case came before the courts, it would seem at first sight that the action of the Belfast trade unionists was very little different from that of the China traders in the earlier case, and that what was legitimate coercion in the business world would also be legitimate in conflicts between labour and employers. This was not the case, however, and such brief references as were made to the earlier decision in the House of Lords were by the way. In the Irish Courts, the majority of the judges failed to see the resemblance between the two situations.

In the Queen's Bench Divisional Court, four of the judges were in favour of dismissing the appeal, and the Chief Baron dissented. The same view was expressed unanimously by the Court of Appeal, and a like fate befell the case in the House of Lords; although the Lord Chancellor, Lord Halsbury, did observe:

> " I do not deny that if some of the observations made in that case, [viz. *Allen v. Flood*], were to be pushed to their logical conclusion, it would be very difficult to resist the Chief Baron's inflexible logic; but with all the respect which any view of that learned judge is entitled to command, and which I unfeignedly entertain, I cannot concur."

Palles thus found himself the sole dissenter in all three Courts, and it will be of interest to ascertain how his " inflexible logic " led him to adopt this view.

The answer lies in his attitude to the two earlier House

8[1898] A.C. 1.

of Lords decisions already mentioned. *Allen v. Flood* was
a clear decision to the effect that it was not actionable for
a single person, not acting in combination with others, to
induce another not to enter into a contract with a third.
The only issue in the *Leathem* case was: did the fact that
the defendants *were* acting in combination make any difference? The Chief Baron admitted that acts not actionable if those of individuals, might become so if done in
concert, but only, he thought, if that combination was a
criminal one—" The criminality of the combination," he
said, " affects the act which is its object."

He then proceeded to examine the *Mogul* case with
meticulous care and he took the view that the *ratio
decidendi* of that case was quite clearly to the effect that
acts done by several persons together, though they cause
loss or harm to another, cannot be made the subject of an
action at law unless the same acts would have been actionable had they been those of one person only. Combining
this with the law laid down in *Allen v. Flood,* where the
acts complained of were substantially similar to those of the
Leathem case, he reached the conclusion that Leathem had
no cause of action.

In so doing, he was influenced decisively by a factor
which was ignored by his brethren—the difficulty of distinguishing the Lisburn case from the earlier *Mogul* case,
albeit that the economic factors involved were entirely different. The other Irish judges, indeed, (or some of them)
thought that the fact that the defendants were trade
unionists introduced some more sinister significance into
their activities, Andrews J., for instance, saying that their
conduct was " more oppressive and capable of becoming
more harmful " than that of the China traders in the
earlier case. In the House of Lords, too, much play was
made on the fact that " numbers may annoy and coerce
where one may not," though the Chief Baron demonstra-
ted the illogicality of this point of view.

A closer analysis of the two cases does little more than
confirm that the views of the Chief Baron were correct.
Both were actions for malicious interference with a right

to carry on a trade. In *Allen v. Flood* there was only one defendant, while in the *Leathem* case there were a number who acted in combination. The several defendants were held liable, but the single one was not.

Two grounds of distinction between the cases have been suggested. In the first place, it has been said that the only ground of distinction was that in the *Leathem* case, illegal means, such as threats, were used, and that the fact that there was a combination was merely incidental and not a ground of distinguishing one from the other (9). Secondly, it is alleged, the distinction lies in the presence or absence of a combination (10), and this appears to have influenced Lord Halsbury in the House of Lords when he refused to concur in Palles's "inflexible logic."

Put in syllogistic form, the Chief Baron's argument appears to run along these lines: Conduct which is not actionable when done by one person cannot become so when done by a combination of persons, unless the combination is criminal and indictable as a conspiracy. The combination in the *Leathem* case was not criminal, because exempted from criminality by the provisions of a statute. Therefore, the conduct of the persons acting in combination is not actionable.

There are two possible answers to the argument. First, that it is irrelevant, because even if there were no combination, the use of illegal means in the Lisburn case distinguished it from *Allen v. Flood* (9). Secondly, it can be said that the Chief Baron's major premiss is invalid, in that it contends that if civil liability depends on the fact of combination, it can only so depend if the combination is criminal and indictable. This was the view expressed by Lord Lindley in the House of Lords when the Lisburn case was before him there. Whether either or both of these objects are valid is not material to the present discussion. What is material is that Palles was prepared to be bound by a chain of reasoning which seemed to him to be logically unanswerable, while Lord Halsbury, while admitting it to

---

⁹*Giblan's Case* [1903] 2 K.B. 600 ; *Pratt v. British Medical Association* [1919] 1 K.B. 244, per McCardie J.
¹⁰*Sorrell v. Smith* [1925] A.C. 700, *per* Lord Dunedin.

be " inflexible," was not prepared to face the consequences of that inflexibility.

The other great case involving these doctrines in which he was engaged was tried before him in Dublin towards the end of his judicial career, in 1912. This was *Larkin v. Long (11)*, which involved the activities of James Larkin and his trade union organisations.

Long was a stevedore in Dublin who, in order to carry out his contracts for the discharge of cargoes, hired dock labourers many of whom were members of the Irish Transport Union of which Larkin was organising secretary. The other Dublin stevedores had formed an association for the purpose of compelling ship-owners to pay higher rates, which the plaintiff had refused to join. The defendants, some of whom were officials of the Transport Union and some of whom were members of the stevedores' association, entered into an agreement to force the plaintiff to join the association, and procured the dock labourers employed by him to break their contracts with him. There was no dispute between Long and his labourers, the dispute being between the former and the association, into which the latter brought Larkin and his union.

The case turned mainly on whether the acts complained of by the plaintiff had been done in furtherance of a trade dispute, and were therefore immune from legal restraint, under the Trade Disputes Act, 1906. Ultimately, the House of Lords was to hold that this was so, and the decisions of both the King's Bench divisional Court and the Court of Appeal in Ireland were reversed.

The actual trial, which took place before the Chief Baron and a special jury, was of considerable interest, and resulted in a verdict for the plaintiff. In his charge to the jury, Palles in dealing with the plaintiff's failure to join the stevedores' association, expressed himself in a way that was indicative of his general views on the subject:

> " Our law is, that a person has a right to exercise his own judgment. It is really in these matters that liberty consists. A person has a right to exercise his own judg-

11[1914] 2 I.R. 285 ; 329.

ment and discretion as to the mode in which he is to earn
his own livelihood in such a way as he likes. A number of
us do a great number of foolish things, and, perhaps, we
would do a great deal better if we followed the advice of
our friends, but in the genius of the Constitution the
matter which is called liberty or freedom in this country is
the right of a man who exercises his own discretion, and it
is only by Act of Parliament that that discretion can be
controlled."

Thus spoke the octogenarian judge, with nearly forty
years' judicial experience behind him. Notions of liberty
and freedom may have changed since 1912, but this
description by Palles can scarcely be surpassed as an
expression of an ideal.

It would be improper to conclude this brief sketch of
the work of Palles the lawyer without making some reference to his contributions in the field of equity. Here again,
the difficulty lies in the application of any principle of
selection, for he took the whole of the jurisdiction of the
Court of Chancery for his province. If one example is to
be taken, it should be from the field of charitable trusts,
in which he displayed a particular mastery of principle.

In an earlier chapter, reference was made to the case of
Attorney-General v. Delany (12), which he had decided in
1875. He had thrown out the suggestion at that time that
in cases of testamentary gifts for the celebration of Masses,
the necessary legal element of " public benefit " might be
supplied if there were a direction for the celebration of
the rite in public. In so doing, he implied that such a gift
could not derive any element of public benefit from any
supposed spiritual efficacy which the religious act might
confer.

In 1896, he reviewed the law once more, in *Attorney-
General v. Hall* (13). There, a testator had bequeathed sums
of money for Masses, giving a direction that there was to
be a public celebration. Palles (with whom the other mem-

¹²I.R. 10 C.L. 104.
¹³[1897] 2 I.R. 426.

bers of the Court concurred) decided that this was a valid and charitable bequest, basing his views on an earlier decision of Lord Chancellor Manners, in 1823.

The final stage had yet to be reached. It had still to be determined whether a case in which there was no such requirement of public celebration would be recognised as charitable. Such a case came before the Court of Appeal in 1906, of which Palles was a member. This was the case of *O'Hanlon v. Logue* (*14*).

In many ways, this was the Chief Baron's judicial masterpiece. Having analysed his attitude in *Delany's Case* thirty years before, he reached the conclusion that his former opinion could not now stand. The common law had held gifts for Masses to be pious because they were gifts to God. Not only were such gifts pious before the Reformation but, had they not been made illegal by statute, they would have been charitable. The illegality only affected the particular mode of performance of such gifts and did not render the gifts non-charitable *per se*. After the Reformation, the gifts would have remained charitable if they had not been made illegal, and when all the laws prohibiting the practice of the Catholic religion were repealed, the effect was to cause such gifts to resume the character they had enjoyed in earlier times and once more become charitable.

Once more, the " inflexible logic " was apparent in every stage of this memorable judgment, and it is possible to follow the Chief Baron step by step in arriving at his conclusions. In the result, the Court decided that a bequest for the celebration of Masses, whether in public or in private, was charitable. This was a decision of the highest Irish tribunal, but the opinion of the House of Lords was not taken thereon. To the present day, indeed, the law in Ireland is governed by *O'Hanlon v. Logue*, but there are indications that, in England, a different view might be taken of the charitable nature of such gifts. This fact may explain the foresight of Palles himself when making his

14[1906] 1 I.R. 247.

will in December, 1916. He included in his will certain bequests for Masses, but was careful to provide that they were to be celebrated in public. From this, one cannot infer any lack of confidence in his own view of the matter; rather, one thinks, he feared lest that view might not be shared across the Irish sea.

From all the cases, a number of facts emerge. In the first place, it can be said, Palles shared with Dr. Johnson the view that " the law is the last result of human wisdom acting upon human experience for the benefit of the public." For him, an examination of the course of precedents must lead to the inexorable conclusion, though where his logic coerced him to dissent from an earlier and non-binding opinion, even when it emanated from himself, he was prepared to do so. Courageous in all things, he did not flinch from the inevitable, for he loved the law as a science for its own sake.

Secondly, there is his all-pervading humility. Sir John Fortescue once wrote that " The judges sit from eight to eleven. They then study the law, read Holy Scripture or use other contemplation at their pleasure." He might have been describing a day in the life of Christopher Palles, who began each day with worship, who imposed upon himself (in a private memorandum drawn up in 1908) the duty of " thinking of God three times daily in Court," and whose whole life was dedicated to the administration of justice. He was eminently a person who believed in the law of nature as being the foundation of all human law. St. Thomas Aquinas taught that no positive enactment of human origin which ran counter to the law of nature could be regarded as law. But St. Thomas was equally adamant on the point that the law of nature is inadequate to the tasks of regulating the affairs of men in society, because of their great diversity. Hence the necessity for human law, a law which Palles applied as a servant, not a master.

Above all, he believed in the fundamental basis of the

common law as being a Christian one. In delivering judgment in his court, he once observed that

> ". . . . . In administering the common law of this country, we are, as I believe us to be, at liberty to remember that it is the law of a Christian country, the growth of centuries of Christian wisdom . . ."

It is in this belief, and in his humility, that the true greatness of Christopher Palles is to be found.

XVI

EPILOGUE

IN his will, which is dated 6th December, 1916, Christopher
Palles, having appointed his niece Elizabeth (Bessie) Palles
as his executrix, went on to state that "the paramount
object of this will is to secure for my son every source of
happiness and comfort consistent with his condition," and,
he added, "I direct that this will shall be construed as
having the attainment of that object my primary intention,
and on which all other provisions . . . shall give way if
necessary." He thereupon devised and bequeathed all his
property to his niece upon trust for his son, and he empowered her to appoint a fit and proper person on her
death to succeed her in the guardianship of the younger
Christopher. His personal estate in the United Kingdom
amounted to the sum of £59,234.

Miss Palles died on 22nd January, 1925, and she, in
turn, bequeathed her personal fortune, some £39,000, upon
trust for the Chief Baron's son. Thereafter, Christopher
lived in England and he died on 2nd January, 1953, in
his ninetieth year. With his passing, the male line of the
family of Palles became extinct, and there is now no
survivor of the name.

APPENDICES

APPENDICES

SUCCESSION LIST OF THE CHANCELLORS, JUSTICES, LAW OFFICERS AND SERJEANTS-AT-LAW IN IRELAND DURING THE PERIOD 1874-1921.

Chancellors

1875. John Thomas Ball.
1880. Thomas, Baron O'Hagan of Tullahogue.
1881. Hugh Law.
1883. Edward Sullivan, Bart.
1885. John Naish.
1885. Edward Gibson, Baron Ashbourne.
1886. John Naish.
1886. Edward Gibson, Baron Ashbourne.
1892. Samuel Walker.
1895. Edward Gibson, Baron Ashbourne.
1905. Samuel Walker, Bart.
1911. Redmond John Barry.
1913. Ignatius John O'Brien, Bart.
1918. James Henry Mussen Campbell, Bart.
1921. John Ross, Bart.

Masters of the Rolls

1870. Edward Sullivan, Bart. (L.C., 1883).
1883. Andrew Marshall Porter, Bart. (ret. 1906).
1906. Richard Edmund Meredith (ret. 1912).
1912. Charles Andrew O'Connor (ret. 1924).

Vice-Chancellor

1867. Hedges Eyre Chatterton (ret. 1904).

Lord Justices of Appeal

1867. Jonathan Christian (ret. 1878).
1878. Rickard Deasy (d. 1883).
1878. Gerald FitzGibbon (d. 1909).
1883. Charles Robert Barry (d. 1897).
1897. Hugh Holmes (ret. 1913).
1909. Richard Robert Cherry (ret. 1916).
1913. John Francis Moriarty (d. 1915).
1915. Stephen Ronan (ret. 1924).
1915. Thomas Francis Molony (ret. 1924).
1918. James O'Connor (ret. 1924).

Justices of the Chancery Division

1878. Stephen Woulfe Flanagan (ret. 1885).
1878. Henry Ormsby (ret. 1885).
1885. John Monroe (ret. 1896).
1896. John Ross, Bart. (ret. 1921).
1904. Dunbar Plunket Barton (ret. 1918).
1918. James O'Connor (ret. 1924).
1918. John Blake Powell (d. 1923).

Judge of the Court of Probate, of the Court of Matrimonial Causes and Matters, and Judge of the Probate Division

1868. Robert Richard Warren (d. 1897).

Chief Justices of the Queen's Bench, and Lord Chief Justices of Ireland

1866. James Whiteside (d. 1876).
1877. George Augustus Chichester May (ret. 1887).
1887. Michael Morris, Bart (to House of Lords, 1889).
1889. Peter, Baron O'Brien of Kilfenora (ret. 1913).
1913. Richard Robert Cherry (ret. 1916).
1916. James Henry Mussen Campbell, Bart. (L. C., 1918).
1918. Thomas Francis Molony, Bart. (ret. 1924).

Justices of the Queen's or King's Bench

1858. James O'Brien (d. 1882).

1861. John David FitzGerald (to House of Lords, 1882).

1872. Charles Robert Barry (d. 1897).

1882. James Anthony Lawson (d. 1887).

1883. William Moore Johnson (ret. 1909).

1883. William O'Brien (from C.P.D.) (d. 1899).

1888. Michael Harrison (d. 1895).

1888. James Murphy (to Ex. D., 1892) (d. 1901).

1888. Hugh Holmes (ret. 1913).

1888. John George Gibson (ret. 1921).

1892. Dodgson Hamilton Madden (ret. 1919).

1897. William Drennan Andrews (ret. 1909).

1897. James Murphy (from Ex. D.) (d. 1901).

1897. Walter Boyd (ret. 1916).

1897. William Kenny (d. 1921).

1900. Dunbar Plunket Barton (to Ch. D., 1905) (ret. 1918).

1901. George Wright (d. 1913).

1907. William Huston Dodd (ret. 1924).

1913. Thomas Francis Molony (ret. 1924).

1915. Jonathan Ernest Pim (ret. 1924).

1916. John Gordon (d. 1922).

1917. William Moore, Bart. (L.C.J., N.I., 1925; d. 1937).

1919. Arthur Warren Samuels (ret. 1924).

Chief Justices of the Common Pleas

1850. James Henry Monahan (ret. 1876).
1876. Michael Morris, Bart. (L.C.J., 1887).

Justices of the Common Pleas

1867. Michael Morris (C.J.C.P., 1876).

1868. James Anthony Lawson (to Q.B.D., 1882).

1878. Michael Harrison (to Q.B.D., 1888).

1882. William O'Brien (to Q.B.D., 1883).

1883. James Murphy (to Q.B.D., 1888).

1887. Hugh Holmes (to Q.B.D., 1888).

Chief Baron of the Exchequer

1874. Christopher Palles (ret. 1916).

Barons of the Court of Exchequer

1859. Francis Alexander FitzGerald (ret. 1882)
1861. Rickard Deasy (L.J., 1878).
1872. Richard Dowse (d. 1890).
1882. William Drennan Andrews (to Q.B.D., 1897).
1892. James Murphy (from Q.B.D.).

Judges of the Court of Bankruptcy

1867. Stearne Ball Miller (d. 1897).
1868. Michael Harrison (to C.P.D., 1878).
1878. Frederick William Walsh (d. 1885).
1885. Walter Boyd (to Q.B.D., 1897).

Judges of the High Court of Admiralty

1867. John FitzHenry Townshend (d. 1893).
1893. William Moore Johnson (ret. 1909).
1910. Dodgson Hamilton Madden (ret. 1919).

Judicial Commissioners, Irish Land Commission

1881. John O'Hagan (ret. 1889).
1890. Edward Falconer Litton (d. 1890).
1890. Edmund T. Bewley (ret. 1898).
1898. Richard Edmund Meredith (M.R., 1906).
1906. James O. Wylie (ret. 1920).
1920. William E. Wylie (ret. 1924).

Attorneys-General

1874. Rt. Hon. John Thomas Ball.
1875. Rt. Hon. Henry Ormsby.
1875. Rt. Hon. George Augustus Chichester May.
1877. Rt. Hon. Edward Gibson.
1880. Rt. Hon. Hugh Law.
1881. Rt. Hon. William Moore Johnson.
1883. Rt. Hon. Andrew Marshall Porter.
1884. Rt. Hon. John Naish.
1885. Rt. Hon. Samuel Walker.
1885. Rt. Hon. Hugh Holmes.
1886. Rt. Hon. Samuel Walker.
1887. Rt. Hon. John George Gibson.
1888. Rt. Hon. Peter O'Brien.
1889. Rt. Hon. Dodgson Hamilton Madden.
1892. Rt. Hon. John Atkinson.
1892. Rt. Hon. The MacDermot.
1895. Rt. Hon. John Atkinson.
1905. Rt. Hon. James Henry Mussen Campbell.
1905. Rt. Hon. Richard Robert Cherry.
1909. Rt. Hon. Redmond John Barry.
1911. Rt. Hon. Charles Andrew O'Connor.
1912. Rt. Hon. Ignatius O'Brien.
1913. Rt. Hon. Thomas Francis Molony.
1913. Rt. Hon. John Francis Moriarty.
1914. Rt. Hon. Jonathan Pim.
1915. Rt. Hon. John Gordon.
1916. Rt. Hon. James Henry Mussen Campbell.
1917. Rt. Hon. James O'Connor.
1918. Rt. Hon. Arthur Warren Samuels.
1919. Rt. Hon. Denis Stanislaus Henry.
1921. Rt. Hon. Thomas Watters Brown.

Solicitors-General

1874. Henry Ormsby.
1875. Hon. David Plunket.
1877. Gerald FitzGibbon.

1878. Hugh Holmes.
1880. William Moore Johnson.
1881. Andrew Marshall Porter.
1883. John Naish.
1883. Samuel Walker.
1885. The MacDermot.
1885. John Monroe.
1885. John George Gibson.
1886. The MacDermot.
1886. John George Gibson.
1887. Peter O'Brien.
1888. Dodgson Hamilton Madden.
1889. John Atkinson.
1892. Edward Carson.
1892. Charles Hare Hemphill.
1895. William Kenny.
1898. Dunbar Plunket Barton.
1900. George Wright.
1901. James Henry Mussen Campbell.
1905. Redmond John Barry.
1909. Charles Andrew O'Connor.
1911. Ignatius O'Brien.
1913. Thomas Francis Molony.
1913. John Francis Moriarty.
1913. Jonathan Pim.
1914. James O'Connor.
1917. James Chambers.
1917. Arthur Warren Samuels.
1918. John Blake Powell.
1918. Denis Stanislaus Henry.
1919. Daniel Martin Wilson.

Serjeants-at-Law

1861. Richard Armstrong.
1865. Colman O'Loghlen, Bart.
1870. David Sherlock.
1877. James Robinson.

1880. Denis Caulfield Heron.
1881. John O'Hagan.
1881. Charles Hare Hemphill.
1884. Peter O'Brien.
1885. John George Gibson.
1885. William Campion.
1887. Dodgson Hamilton Madden.
1888. Hewitt Poole Jellett.
1892. William Huston Dodd.
1907. Charles Andrew O'Connor.
1907. Matthew J. Bourke.
1908. John Francis Moriarty.
1909. Ignatius J. O'Brien.
1911. Thomas Francis Molony.
1911. Charles L. Matheson.
1912. Alexander Martin Sullivan.
1913. George McSweeney.
1919. Henry Hanna.

APPENDIX II.

SUCCESSION LIST OF THE JUSTICES AND LAW OFFICERS IN IRELAND DURING THE PERIOD 1921-1960.

Northern Ireland

Lord Chief Justices of Northern Ireland

1921. Denis Stanislaus Henry, Bart. (d. 1925)
1925. William Moore, Bart. (ret. 1937) (d. 1944)
1937. James Andrews, Bart. (d. 1951)
1951. John Clarke, Baron MacDermott of Belmont.

Lord Justices of Appeal

1921. William Moore. (L.C.J. N.I., 1925)
1921. James Andrews. (L.C.J. N.I., 1937)
1925. Richard Best. (d. 1938)
1937. Anthony Brutus Babington, Kt. (ret. 1949)
1939. Edward Sullivan Murphy. (d. 1945)
1946. Samuel Clarke Porter. (d. 1956)
1949. Arthur Black.
1956. Lancelot Ernest Curran.

Justices of the High Court of Justice

1921. Daniel Martin Wilson. (d. 1931)
1922. Thomas Watters Brown. (d. 1944)
1932. Robert Dick Megaw. (ret. 1943) (d. 1947)
1943. Arthur Black.
1944. John Clarke MacDermott. (to House of Lords, 1947)
1947. William Lowry. (ret. 1949)
1949. Charles Leo Sheil.
1949. Lancelot Ernest Curran.
1956. Herbert Andrew McVeigh.

Attorneys-General

1921. Rt. Hon. Richard Best.

1925. Rt. Hon. Anthony Brutus Babington.

1937. Edward Sullivan Murphy.

1939. Arthur Black.

1941. Rt. Hon. John Clarke MacDermott.

1944. Rt. Hon. William Lowry.

1947. Lancelot Ernest Curran.

1949. Rt. Hon. John Edmond Warnock.

1956. Rt. Hon. William Brian Maginnis.

Southern Ireland, the Irish Free State and the Republic of Ireland.

Chief Justices of Southern Ireland, the Irish Free State and of Ireland.

1921. Thomas Francis Molony, Bart. (ret. 1924)

1924. Hugh Kennedy. (d. 1936)

1936. Timothy Sullivan. (d. 1946)

1946. Conor Alexander Maguire.

Lord Justices of Appeal in Southern Ireland and the Irish Free State.

1915. Stephen Ronan. (ret. 1924) (d. 1925)

1918. James O'Connor, Kt. (ret. 1924) (d. 1932)

Presidents of the High Court of Justice.

1924. Timothy Sullivan.

1936. Conor Alexander Maguire.

1946. George Gavan Duffy. (d. 1951)

1951. Cahir Davitt.

Justices of the Supreme Court of Justice.

1924. Charles Andrew O'Connor. (ret. 1925) (d. 1928)
1924. Gerald FitzGibbon. (ret. 1938) (d. 1942)
1925. James Augustine Murnaghan. (ret. 1954)
1936. James Creed Meredith. (d. 1942)
1936. James Geoghegan. (ret. 1950) (d. 1951)
1939. William John Johnston. (ret. 1940) (d. 1940)
1940. John O'Byrne. (d. 1954)
1942. William Black. (ret. 1951)
1950. Cecil Lavery.
1951. Theodore Conyngham Kingsmill Moore.
1953. Carroll O'Daly.
1954. Martin Cyril Maguire.

Justices of the High Court of Justice in Southern Ireland
and the Irish Free State, 1921-1924.

1907. William Huston Dodd. (ret. 1924) (d. 1930)
1915. Jonathan Pim. (ret. 1924)
1919. Arthur Warren Samuels. (ret. 1924)
1912. Charles Andrew O'Connor, M.R. (ret. 1925) (d. 1928)
1918. John Blake Powell. (d. 1923)

Justices of the High Court of Justice in the Irish Free
State and the Republic of Ireland, 1924-1960.

1924. James Creed Meredith.
1924. Thomas Lopdell O'Shaughnessy. (ret. 1925) (d. 1933)
1924. William John Johnston.
1924. James Augustine Murnaghan.
1924. Henry Hanna. (ret. 1943) (d. 1945)
1924. William E. Wylie. (ret. 1936)
1926. John O'Byrne.
1936. Conor Alexander Maguire.
1936. George Gavan Duffy.
1939. William Black.
1940. Martin Cyril Maguire.
1942. Kevin O'Hanrahan Haugh.

1943. Andrew Kingsbury Overend. (d. 1947)
1945. Cahir Davitt.
1946. Kevin Joseph Dixon. (d. 1959)
1947. Theodore Conyngham Kingsmill Moore.
1951. Charles Francis Casey. (d. 1952)
1951. Frederick Gardner Orford Budd.
1952. Richard McLoughlin.
1954. George D. Murnaghan.
1954. Thomas Teevan.
1959. Brian Walsh.

Attorneys-General

1922. Hugh Kennedy. (Law Officer, 1922-23)
1924. John O'Byrne.
1926. John A. Costello.
1932. Conor Alexander Maguire.
1936. James Geoghegan.
1936. Patrick Lynch. (ret. 1940)
1940. Kevin O'Hanrahan Haugh.
1942. Kevin Joseph Dixon.
1946. Carroll O'Daly.
1948. Cecil Lavery.
1950. Charles Francis Casey.
1951. Carroll O'Daly.
1953. Thomas Teevan.
1954. Andrew O'Keeffe.
1955. Patrick McGilligan.
1957. Andrew O'Keeffe.

APPENDIX III.

BIBLIOGRAPHY.

I.—*Manuscript Materials* :

    1.—The Library of King's Inns, Dublin :
        Minutes of the Benchers, 1872-1920.
        Admission Books.
        Minutes of the Home Circuit, 1782-1885.

    2.—The Irish Land Commission :
        County of Cavan :   Estate of Eleanor Bruce
        Pratt, [Record No. 1883].

    3.—The Library of the Queen's University of Belfast :
        Hamilton Letters, 1889-1912.
        Hamilton Papers, 1879-1923.

    4.—The Library of University College, Dublin :
        MS volume of judgments in *Palles Library*.

    5.—The Palles Papers [In the custody of Mrs. Irma Bruce
        Waddell].

II.—*Newspapers and Periodicals* :

    The Belfast Newsletter.
    The Clongownian.
    The Dublin University Magazine.
    The Derry Journal.
    The Freeman's Journal.
    The Green Bag.
    Irish Law Times and Solicitors Journal.
    Ireland.
    The Irish Times.
    New Irish Jurist and Local Government Review.
    The Northern Whig.
    The Pall Mall Gazette.
    T.C.D.
    The Times.
    Zoz.

III.—*Parliamentary Papers* :

Select Committee on Legal Education. Report 1846. H.C. 1846 (686) x, 1-534.

Royal Commission on the University of Dublin and Trinity College, Dublin. H.C. 1853 (1837) xiv, 1-502.

Correspondence between a Committee of the Irish Bar and the Irish Government, 1870 (415), lvii, 305.

Report of the King's Inns, Dublin, Inquiry Commission as to sums received in the admission of Attorneys and Solicitors, as deposits for chambers, etc., 1872 [C. 486] xx, 739.

Royal Commission on University Education in Ireland. Appendix to the 2nd Report. Minutes of Evidence, 1902. (Cd. 900) xxxi, 463.

Royal Commission on Trinity College, Dublin, and the University of Dublin. Appendix to the 1st Report, 1906. [Cd. 3176]. Final Report. 1907. [Cd. 3311]. Appendix to the Final Report ; Minutes of Evidence and Documents. 1907. [Cd. 3312]. xii, 87.

Universities and Colleges (Ireland). Final Report of the Dublin Commissioners, 1911. [Cd. 5877], xxi, 485. *Ibid.* Report of the Belfast Commissioners, 1911. [Cd. 5929], xxi, 499.

IV.—*Printed Materials* :

Annual Register, 1831-1920. London.

Bailey, K.C.: *A History of Trinity College, Dublin, 1892-1945.* Dublin, 1947.

Ball, F. E.: *The Judges in Ireland, 1221-1921.* 2 Vols. London, 1926.

Blackburne, E.: *Francis Blackburne.* London. 1874.

Bodkin, M. McD.: *Recollections of an Irish Judge.* London. 1914.

Burtchaell, G. D., and Sadleir, T. U. : *Alumni Dublinenses, 1583-1860*. Dublin. 1935.

Burke, O. J.: *Anecdotes of the Connaught Circuit, from 1604 to the close of the present time*. Dublin. 1885.

—— *History of the Lord Chancellors of Ireland, A.D. 1186-A.D. 1874*. London and Dublin. 1879.

Campbell, T. J.: *Fifty Years of Ulster, 1890-1940*. Belfast. 1941.

Corcoran, J.: *The Clongowes Record, 1814-1932*. Dublin. n.d.

Craig, M. J.: *Dublin, 1660-1860*. London 1952

Curran, J. Adye (Judge): *Recollections*. London. 1915.

Curran, J. P.: *Sketches of the Irish Bar*. London. 1855.

Derriman, J.: *The Pageantry of the Law*. London. 1955.

Dictionary of National Biography, *Supplement, 1912-21*. London. 1927.

Duhigg, B. J.: *King's Inns, Dublin*. Dublin. 1806.

Edge, John: *Recollections*. London. 1915.

Eversley, Lord : *Gladstone and Ireland*. London. 1912.

Gamble, Charles : *Solicitors in Ireland, 1607-1921*. Dublin. 1921.

Gilbert, Rosa Mulholland: *Life of Sir John T. Gilbert*. London. 1905.

Gwynn, D.: *John Redmond*. London. 1932.

Hale, L.: *Life of John Philpot Curran*. London. 1958.

Hamilton, G. E.: *The King's Inns, Dublin*. Dublin. 1915.

Hammond, J. L.: *Gladstone and the Irish Nation*. London. 1938.

Healy, M.: *The Old Munster Circuit*. Dublin. 1939.

Healy, T. M.: *Letters and Leaders of My Day*. 2 vols. London. 1928.

Hicks-Beach, V.: *Sir Michael Hicks-Beach*. 2 vols. London. 1932.

Holland, B.: *Life of 8th Duke of Devonshire*. 2 vols. London. 1917.

Hyde, H. Montgomery : *Carson*. London. 1953.

Incorporated Law Society of Ireland, Record of the Centenary of the Charter, 1852-1952. Dublin. 1953.

Jefferson, H.: *Viscount Pirrie of Belfast*. Belfast. 1947.

Lefroy, T.: *Memoir of Chief Justice Lefroy*. Dublin. 1871.

Littledale, W. F.: *The Society of King's Inns*. Dublin. 1859. (pamphlet).

Locker-Lampson, G.: *A Consideration of the State of Ireland in the 19th Century*. London. 1907.

McDowell, R. B.: *Public Opinion and Government Policy in Ireland, 1801-1846*. London. 1952.

McGrath, F.: *Newman's University*. London. 1951.

MacKinnon, Sir Frank : *On Circuit*. London. 1940.

McKnight, T.: *Ulster As It Is*. 2 vols. London. 1896.

MacNeill, J. G. S.: *What I have Seen and Heard*. London. 1925.

Marjoribanks, E.: *Lord Carson*. Vol. 1. London. 1932.

Maxwell, C.: *A History of Trinity College, Dublin, 1591-1892*. Dublin. 1946.

Moody, T. W. and Beckett, J. C.: *Queen's Belfast, 1845-1949.*. 2 vols. London. 1959.

Morley, J.: *Life of Gladstone*. 2 vols. London.

Recollections. 2 vols. London. 1905.

Morris, W. O'Connor: *Memories and Thoughts of Life*. London. 1895.

Ireland, 1798-1898. London. 1898.

O'Brien, R. Barry : *Charles Stewart Parnell*. 2 vols. London. 1899.

Dublin Castle and the Irish People. London. 1912.

O'Brien, C. Cruise: *Parnell and his Party*. London. 1957.

O'Brien, Lord : *Reminiscences*. (Ed. Hon. Georgina

O'Brien). London. 1916.

O'Connor, Sir James : *History of Ireland, 1798-1924.* 2 vols. London. 1925.

O'Connor, T. P.: *The Parnell Movement.* London. 1886.

O'Flaherty, L.: *T. M. Healy.* London. 1927.

O'Flanagan, J. R.: *The Irish Bar.* London. 1879.

—— *The Munster Circuit.* London. 1880.

O'Shaughnessy, M. S.: *Legal Education in Ireland.* 1872. (pamphlet).

Porter, F. T.: *Gleanings and Reminiscences.* Dublin. 1875.

"Rhadamanthus": *Our Judges.* Dublin. 1890.

Ross, Sir John : *The Years of My Pilgrimage.* London. 1924.

Pilgrim Scrip. London. 1927.

Sheehy, E. (Judge): *May It Please the Court.* Dublin. 1951.

Shiel, R. L.: *Legal and Political Sketches.* 2 vols. London. 1855.

Smith, G. H.: *The North East Bar.* Belfast. 1910.

Somerville, E. Œ. and Ross, M.: *An Incorruptible Irishman.* London. 1932.

Sullivan, A. M.: *New Ireland.* London. 1884.

Sullivan, A. M. (Serjeant): *Old Ireland.* London. 1927.

The Last Serjeant. London. 1952.

Thom's Directory of Ireland.

Walsh, J. E.: *Ireland Ninety Years Ago.* Dublin. 1876.

Walsh, P. J.: *Archbishop Walsh.* Dublin. 1928.

White, T. de V.: *The Road of Excess.* Dublin. 1946.

Whiteside, J.: *Early Sketches of Eminent Persons.* Dublin. 1870.

Wynne, M.: *An Irishman and his Family.* London. 1937.

INDEX

INDEX